HARMONY
BAROQUE TO CONTEMPORARY

PART I

R. EVAN COPLEY

PROFESSOR OF MUSIC
UNIVERSITY of NORTHERN COLORADO

Copyright © 1978, 1991
STIPES PUBLISHING L.L.C.

ISBN 0-87563-373-0

Published by

STIPES PUBLISHING L.L.C.
202-204 West University Avenue
Post Office Box 526
Champaign, Illinois 61824-0526

Preface to the Second Edition

Harmony-Baroque to Contemporary, Part I is concerned with music fundamentals, and with the writing of basic diatonic harmony in small homophonic forms. It is intended for use at the secondary or college level to provide projects for one academic year. Each chapter includes discussion, analysis, then application (written and keyboard assignments) of the concepts of musical styles.

Considerable Baroque and Classic literature has been included in *Part I,* and it can be used for analysis beyond that specifically asked for in the assignment sections, as time allows. The harmonic and structural materials presented in *Part I* (and in *Part II*) are descriptive of much of the music being performed in concerts, and being taught in private studio lessons. .

In *Part I,* chapters have been included that give brief, general descriptions of the Baroque and Classic periods. Although the Classic period is introduced in Chapter 21, it is not assumed that at this point the student knows all there is to know about the Baroque style. The Classic style is introduced at this point to give a greater variety to the written assignments. Since the differences between Baroque and Classic styles are more a matter of texture and form than of harmonic vocabulary, Baroque and Classic examples and assignments are used from Chapter 21, forward.

The brief history and form sections in this book are not intended to replace detailed and thorough courses in those subjects. The history sections are included to provide a time framework for the theoretical materials. The form sections provide formal models (designs) into which the student can shape harmony in his or her compositions.

The students should practice sight-singing exercises from another source which generally coincide with the projects under discussion in written and keyboard theory. (There are several fine sight-singing texts available.) It is recommended that students practice using the basic conducting patterns while they are sight-singing.

Ear-training exercises which are correlated to the chapters in *Part I* are provided in Appendix V.

The keyboard assignments in the text require little piano technique, and they are not intended to enhance technique. They are important because they provide the student with a visual, spatial image of the scales, intervals, and triads that will accelerate learning and facilitate retention of the material.

This text is not intended to produce professional composers. However, it is hoped that it will aid in the training of teachers, performers, and conductors who will better understand musical styles; who can learn music more efficiently; and who will then teach, perform, and conduct music with greater sensitivity. Students concentrating in music composition should benefit from understanding the basic elements of eighteenth, nineteenth, and twentieth *(Part II)* century styles. These studies will help them to acquire technique on which to begin developing a personal style.

I am grateful to my students and colleagues who have, during the past three decades, asked questions and made suggestions that have helped shape these books.

R. Evan Copley
Professor of Music
University of Northern Colorado
Greeley, Colorado
1991

Table of Contents

CHAPTER 1

Notation

The *staff* as we now know it is a further development of the four-line staff which evolved during the tenth and eleventh centuries. The eleventh century staff was one of four lines, having either C or F designated with an appropriate *clef*.

Example 1-a

The staff in general use since the thirteenth century is the five-line staff shown below. Although a wide variety of clef designations are possible, many of them are seldom encountered, and their meaning can quickly be deduced from the understanding of the following clefs:

Example 1-b   *Treble clef* or G clef

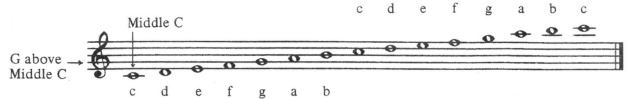

Example 1-c   *Alto clef* or C clef (used principally by the viola).

Example 1-d   *Tenor clef* or C clef (used for the upper ranges of the bassoon, trombone, and cello).

Example 1-e   *Bass clef* or F clef

Observe that two dots are placed on either side of the F line.

Example 1-f The *Grand Staff*

Added lines above or below the staff are called *ledger lines*. When the number of ledger lines exceeds three or four, the composer or arranger will generally employ a higher or lower clef, as needed. The 8 or 8va sign may be used above the treble clef or below the bass clef for notes requiring more than three or four ledger lines.

Example 1-g

A *sharp* (♯) placed before (to the left of) a note raises that note one half-step. A *flat* (♭) placed before a note lowers that note one half-step. The *natural* sign (♮) cancels all sharps and flats and *double sharps* (×) and *double flats* (♭♭) which otherwise would affect that line or space. In order to cancel a flat, a natural (not a sharp) is used. Likewise, in order, to cancel a sharp, a natural (not a flat) is used.

Enharmonic equivalents are notes which are written differently, but sound the same (on the piano).

Example 1-h

enharmonic equivalents

An *accidental* (♯, ♭, ♮, ×, or ♭♭) placed before a note affects that note throughout that measure and is cancelled by the bar line. (This principle was not uniformly and consistently applied by musicians prior to 1750.) The bar line does not cancel an accidental placed before a tied note. In example 1-i the second note is still e♭.

Example 1-i

The composer's intention concerning the third note in example 1-i should be shown.

A sharp placed before a note sharped in the key signature does not result in a double sharped note; the sharp is precautionary.

Example 1-j

still f♯, not f×

3

If a flatted note is to be sharped later in the same measure, it is not necessary to precede the sharp with a natural.

Example 1-k

If a double sharped note is to be a sharped note later in the same measure, it is not necessary to precede the sharp with a natural, although this was done in nineteenth and early twentieth century publications.

Example 1-l

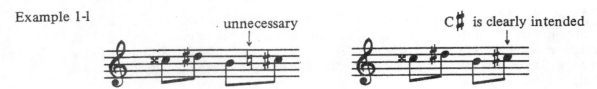

If a double flatted note is to be a flat note later in the same measure, it is not necessary to precede the flat with a natural.

Example 1-m

A natural cancels both sharps in a double sharped note, and a natural cancels both flats in a double flatted note.

Example 1-n

Keyboard Assignment 1

Locate the following notes on the piano keyboard.

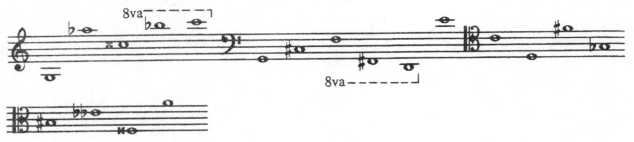

CHAPTER 2

Intervals--Unisons and Seconds

An *interval* is the distance between two notes, counting in alphabetical succession both notes and any notes in between them. An interval is said to be *harmonic* when the two tones sound simultaneously and *melodic* when the tones sound in succession.

Example 2-a

harmonic intervals   melodic intervals

A *perfect unison* (P1) occurs when two (or more) tone-producing agents sound the same pitch.

Example 2-b

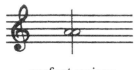

perfect unison

A *half-step* is the smallest interval found between any two adjacent keys on a keyboard.

Example 2-c

half-steps

A *whole-step* is the interval which includes two adjacent half-steps.

Example 2-d

whole-steps

A *minor second* (m2) is half-step which is written using alphabetically adjacent notes.

Example 2-e

minor seconds

A *major second* (M2) is a whole-step which is written using alphabetically adjacent notes.

Example 2-f

major seconds

An *augmented unison* (A1) is a half-step written using the same letter for both notes, one note being inflected up or down by means of an accidental.

Example 2-g

augmented unisons

An *augmented second* (A2) is a second which includes three half-steps.

Example 2-h

augmented seconds

A *diminished second* (d2) (rare) is one half-step smaller than a minor second, and is enharmonically equivalent to a perfect unison.

Example 2-i

diminished second

If no sharps or flats are present, all of the seconds on a staff are major seconds except two: b to c and e to f, which are minor seconds.

Example 2-j

major seconds

Keyboard Assignment 2

Play and name augmented, major, or minor seconds above or below any given note.

6

CHAPTER 3
The Major Scale

A *scale* is an alphabetical succession of tones. In the major scale that composers of the eighteenth and nineteenth centuries used in much of their music, the intervals between adjacent notes fall into the pattern: M2 M2 m2 M2 M2 M2 m2. Minor seconds occur between the third and fourth steps and between the seventh and eighth steps. All other steps are major seconds. The first and eighth steps have the same letter name and inflection (sharp, flat, or natural).

Example 3-a

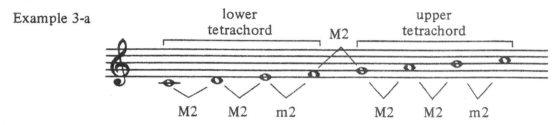

The arrangement of the major and minor seconds in the lower *tetrachord* (lower four scale degrees) is duplicated in the upper tetrachord, with a major second occurring between the tetrachords.

The major scale's arrangement of major and minor seconds can be duplicated using any note as the first scale degree by using sharps or flats to maintain the interval pattern. For example, to write a major scale on D♭ :

1. Write an alphabetical succession of tones, beginning on D and add a flat before each D.

2. Examine each interval, beginning with the interval between steps one and two.

3. Add flats to correct the interval pattern.

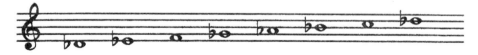

Keyboard Assignment 3

Play major scales beginning on the following notes: D♭ , E♭ , G♭ , A♭ , B♭ , D, E, F, G, A, and B. "Correct" piano fingerings are not relevant to this assignment.

CHAPTER 4
Fifths, Circle of Fifths, Key Signatures

An interval of a *fifth* is the distance between the first and last notes of five alphabetically succeeding tones.

Example 4-a.

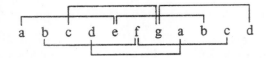

A *perfect fifth* (P5) is the interval found between the first and fifth steps of a major scale. A perfect fifth contains the equivalent of three whole-steps and a half-step.

Example 4-b

D Major   E♭ Major

A *diminished fifth* (d5) contains three whole-steps or their equivalent. An augmented fifth (A5) contains four whole-steps.

Example 4-c

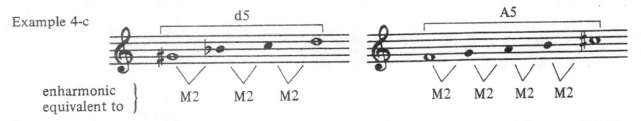

When no sharps or flats are used, all the fifths on the staff are perfect, except the fifth between b and f, which is diminished.

Example 4-d

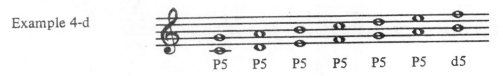

A fifth which is perfect on the staff remains perfect when both notes are raised or lowered an equal distance.

Example 4-e

A fifth which is perfect on the staff becomes diminished when the distance between the notes is decreased by one half-step.

Example 4-f

P5   d5   d5   d5   d5

The diminished fifth, b - f, remains diminished when both notes are raised or lowered an equal distance.

Example 4-g

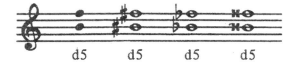

d5   d5   d5   d5

The diminished fifth, b - f, can be made perfect by increasing the distance between the two notes by one half-step.

Example 4-h

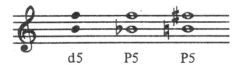

d5   P5   P5

The *circle of fifths* in example 4-i is a visual representation of the major keys and their signatures. Each succeeding key signature (moving clockwise around the circle) includes one sharp more or one flat fewer than did the adjacent key in the series. The key signature for each key is shown in both the treble and bass clefs.

Example 4-i

Circle of Fifths

Flats and sharps are added to the alto and tenor clefs in the following patterns.

Example 4-j

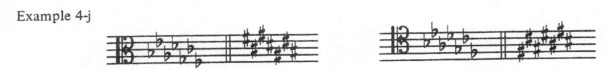

(There is no specific keyboard assignment for this chapter.)

CHAPTER 5

Intervals

Intervals may be classified into two general types: the perfect intervals and the imperfect intervals. The perfect intervals are unisons, fourths, fifths, and octaves. The imperfect intervals are the seconds, thirds, sixths, and sevenths.

The *perfect* intervals may be diminished, perfect, or augmented.[1]

Example 5−a

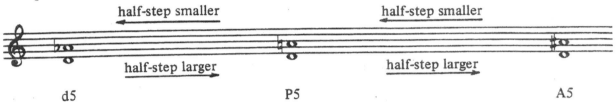

The *imperfect* intervals may generally be diminished, minor, major, or augmented.

Example 5−b

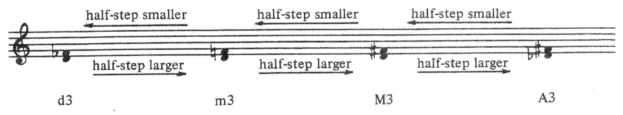

Usually the perfect intervals are not written enharmonically as augmented or diminished imperfect intervals, as in the case of the augmented third above. Although the augmented third is enharmonically equivalent to a perfect fourth, the movement of the voices could make such notation logical, as in example 5−c.

Example 5−c

The Perfect Intervals

Unisons and *fifths* have been discussed in the previous chapters.

The *perfect fourth* includes two major seconds and a minor second. When no sharps or flats are present, all of the fourths on the staff are perfect except the fourth from F to B, which is augmented.

---

[1] In rare instances, the fourth may be doubly augmented.

Example 5—d

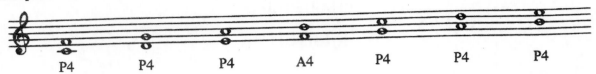

P4   P4   P4   A4   P4   P4   P4

A fourth which is perfect on the staff remains perfect when both notes are raised or lowered equally.

Example 5—e

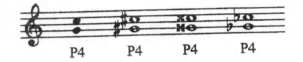

P4   P4   P4   P4

A fourth which is perfect on the staff becomes augmented when the distance between the notes is increased by one half-step.

Example 5—f

P4   A4   A4

The *augmented fourth* and *diminished fifth* are enharmonic equivalents. Because they both encompass the distance of three whole-steps, or their equivalents, the augmented fourth and diminished fifth are both often designated the *"tritone."*

Example 5—g

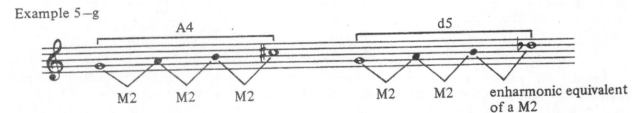

A4   d5

M2   M2   M2   M2   M2   enharmonic equivalent of a M2

The augmented fourth, F to B, is made perfect by decreasing the distance between them by one half-step.

Example 5—h

A4   P4   P4

The distance from the first scale degree to the fourth scale degree in a major scale is a perfect fourth.

Example 5—i

P4

F Major

12

The Imperfect Intervals

Seconds have been discussed in Chapter 2.

A *major third* (M3) includes two major seconds, and a *minor third* (m3) includes a major second and a minor second.

Example 5–j

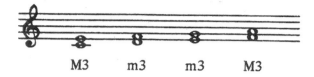

The distance from the first scale degree to the third scale degree in a major scale is a major third.

Example 5–k

F♯ Major

The *major sixth* (M6) is a major second larger than a perfect fifth; the *minor sixth* (m6) is a minor second larger than a perfect fifth. An *augmented sixth* is a minor second larger than a major sixth.

Example 5–l

The sixth degree of a major scale is a major sixth above the first degree.

Example 5–m

E Major

Sevenths may be major, minor, or diminished. The seventh scale degree of a major scale is a *major seventh* above the first scale degree.

Example 5–n

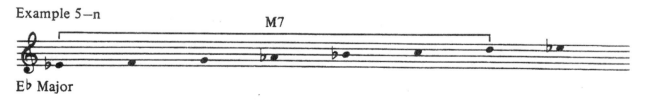

E♭ Major

The *minor seventh* is a major second smaller than an octave.

Example 5–o

13

The *augmented sixth* and the minor seventh are enharmonic equivalents.

Example 5—p

The major sixth and *diminished seventh* are enharmonic equivalents.

Example 5—q

All the intervals above the first scale degree in a major scale are either perfect or major.

Example 5—r

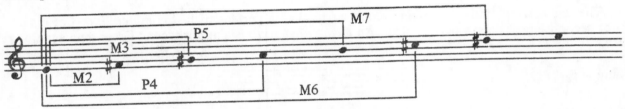

Inversion of Intervals

Intervals are said to be inverted when the notes are reversed in respect to highest and lowest.

Example 5—s

An interval, when inverted, becomes a new interval whose general type may be found by subtracting the original interval from the number nine. Thus, when inverted, sevenths become seconds, sixths become thirds, fifths become fourths, and so on. When intervals are inverted, perfect intervals remain perfect, as in example 5—s. Diminished intervals become augmented and augmented intervals become diminished, when inverted.

Example 5—t

14

Minor intervals become major and major intervals become minor, when inverted.

Example 5—u

m6   M3   M3   m6

Keyboard Assignment 5

Play any interval above or below any given note.

CHAPTER 6
Minor Scales

A *minor scale* is a direct alphabetical succession of tones having a minor third between the first and third scale degrees. In key signatures, sharps and flats in minor keys are placed on the staff in the same order as in major keys. Thus, any key signature may be used for both a minor key or for a major key and the two keys are said to be *related*.

The *minor key* which is related to a major key is represented by the sixth scale degree of the major key. Thus, the first scale degree, the *tonic*, of a minor key is a minor third below the tonic of its related major. The related major of a minor key is a minor third above the tonic of the minor key.

Example 6—a

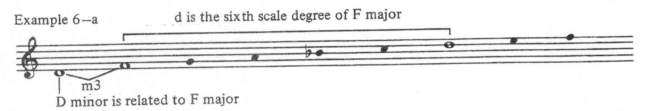

D minor is related to F major

A scale on D, for example, using the key signature of F major, is designated D *natural minor*; or D minor, *pure form*. (This scale is also known as the *aeolian mode* on D.)

Example 6—b

D natural minor

The *harmonic minor scale* is formed by raising, by a half-step, the seventh scale degree of the natural minor scale (both ascending and descending).

Example 6—c

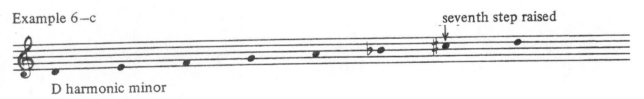

D harmonic minor

The *melodic minor scale* is formed by raising, by a half-step, the sixth and seventh scale degrees of the natural minor scale as the scale ascends, and returning the sixth and seventh scale degrees to natural minor as the scale descends.

Example 6—d

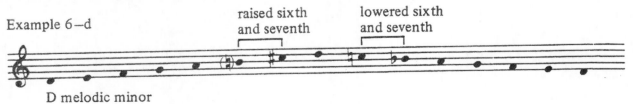

D melodic minor

The *harmonic minor* scale is so named because the composers of the seventeenth, eighteenth, and nineteenth centuries consistently raised the seventh scale degree in harmonic passages similar to example 6—e.

Example 6—e

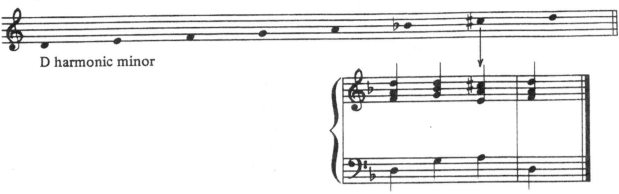

D harmonic minor

The *melodic minor* scale, like the harmonic minor scale, is a theoretical concept rooted in actual musical practice. Composers and performers of the seventeenth and eighteenth centuries probably found the augmented second which occurs between the sixth and seventh scale degrees difficult to sing or play in tune when this interval was used melodically in a vocal or instrumental part. The use of the melodic minor scale avoids the augmented second.

Example 6—f shows the circle of fifths with major keys outside and their related minor keys inside the circle.

Example 6—f

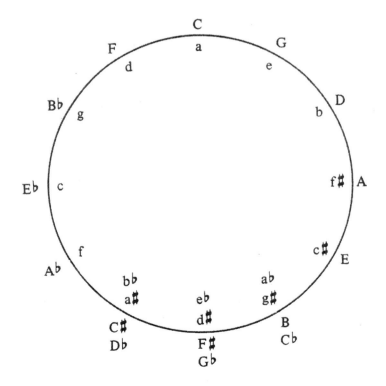

Example 6—g illustrates various natural, harmonic, and melodic minor scales and their key signatures. (Scales not included in this example are the subject of the written exercises which conclude this chapter.)

Example 6—g

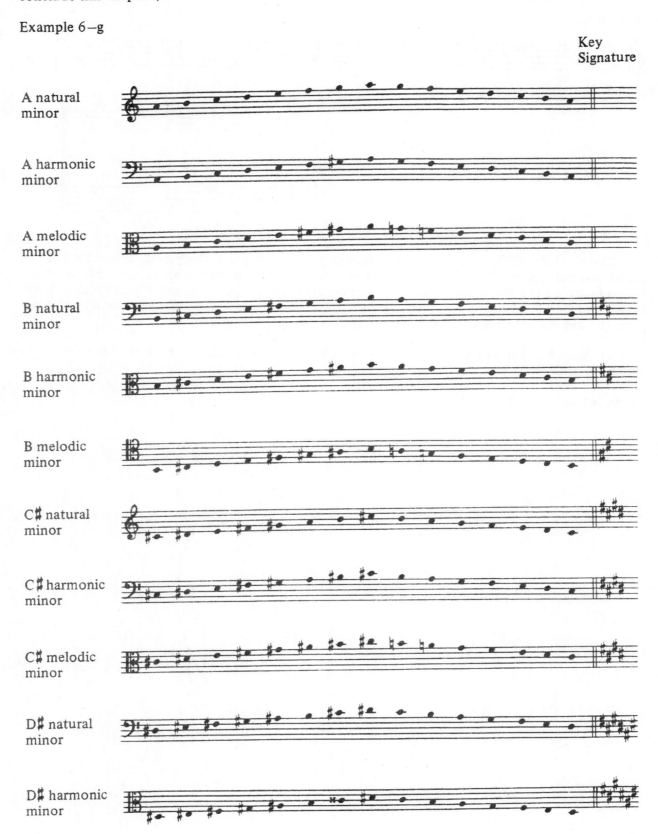

(Example 6–g cont.)

Key
Signature

D# melodic
minor

Bb natural
minor

Bb harmonic
minor

Bb melodic
minor

C natural
minor

C harmonic
minor

C melodic
minor

D natural
minor

D harmonic
minor

D melodic
minor

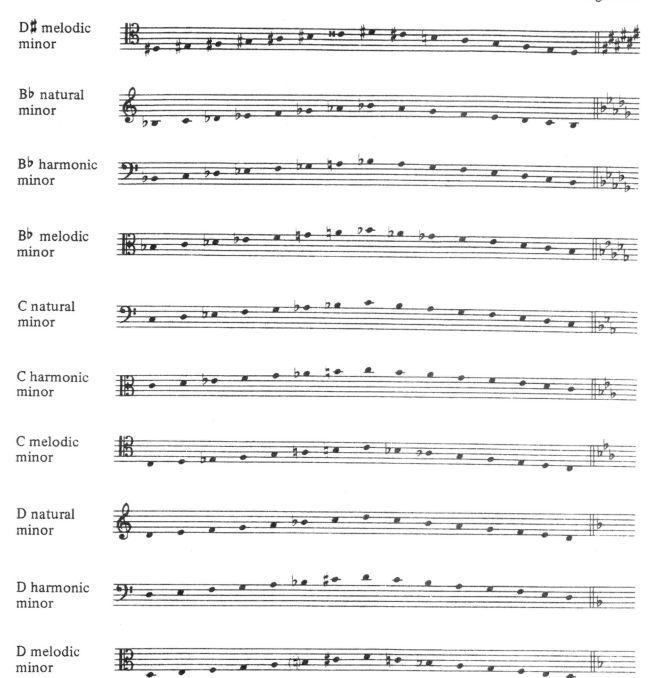

Keyboard Assignment 6

Play any natural, harmonic, or melodic minor scale ascending and descending. (Speed and "correct" piano fingerings are not relevant to this assignment.)

19

CHAPTER 7
Rhythm

Rhythm is concerned with the organization of music as it occurs in time, including the duration of notes and rests, the periodic recurrence of strong and weak accents or beats, and in a larger sense, the form or shape of the musical work as a whole.

Tempo refers to the rate of the beat or pulse in a piece of music.

The *bar line* is a vertical line which divides a staff into *measures*.

Example 7—a

bar line   measure

The *notes* and *rests* used in the music from the sixteenth century to the present are arranged on the staffs below in decreasing order of value.

Example 7—b (notes)

Notes: breve double whole half quarter eighth sixteenth thirty- sixtyfourth
              whole   second

equal in
value

Example 7—c (rests)

Rests: breve   whole   half   quarter   eighth   sixteenth   thirtysecond   sixtyfourth

The *whole-rest* is used to indicate a whole measure of rest in any meter, although sometimes the breve rest is used in $\frac{4}{2}$.

A *dot* following a note increases the note's value by half. Two dots following a note increase the value of the note by three-fourths. Observe in Example 7—d, that if a note on a line is dotted, the dot is placed in the space *above* the line.

Rests may also be dotted and doubly dotted.

A *tie* placed between two notes of the same pitch extends the sound of the first note to include the value of both notes.

Example 7—d

The *unit* is that note or its equivalent value which occupies the time of one actual beat. The *division* is the note into which the unit regularly divides. The unit may regularly divide into two equal parts (simple meter) or into three equal parts (compound meter). The *subdivision* is the note into which the division regularly divides. The division regularly divides into two equal parts in both simple and compound meters.

Example 7—e

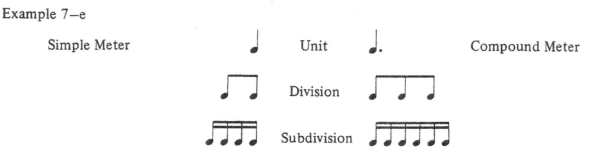

Example 7—m shows that there are many types of notes which can serve as the unit value. The composer's decision to use, for example, $\frac{6}{8}$ (dotted quarter-note as the unit) rather than $\frac{6}{4}$ (dotted half-note as the unit) is purely arbitrary; it will in no way affect the sound of the music, since $\frac{6}{8}$ is not necessarily faster than $\frac{6}{4}$.

Time signature and *meter* are terms which are often used interchangeably. Time signatures are the two numbers, one above the other, which are found at the beginning of a piece of music, and which indicate the meter. The time signature indicates the number of note values possible in a measure of the music, and the probable arrangement of the divisions of the beat.

Example 7—f

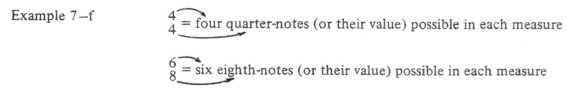

$\frac{4}{4}$ = four quarter-notes (or their value) possible in each measure

$\frac{6}{8}$ = six eighth-notes (or their value) possible in each measure

Meter results from recurring patterns of *primary accents* (strong), *secondary accents* (weak), and *unaccented* beats. All measures in a meter will regularly contain like patterns of accents, the first beat generally having the strongest accent.

Example 7—g

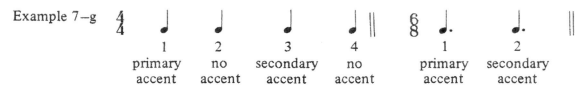

Meter classification is necessary for proper performance of any meter. Meter classification is determined by the number of divisions of the unit (whether it is simple or compound) and the number of units present in each measure. Some common meter classifications are shown in example 7—h.

21

Example 7—h

Duple Simple (D.S.)	$\frac{2}{4}, \frac{2}{2}$	Quadruple Simple (Quad.S.)	$\frac{4}{4}, \frac{4}{2}$
Duple Compound (D.C.)	$\frac{6}{8}, \frac{6}{4}$	Quadruple Compound (Quad.C.)	$\frac{12}{4}, \frac{12}{8}$
Triple Simple (T.S.)	$\frac{3}{4}, \frac{3}{8}$	Quintuple Simple (Quin.S.)	$\frac{5}{4}, \frac{5}{2}$
Triple Compound (T.C.)	$\frac{9}{8}, \frac{9}{16}$	Mixed (M.)	$\frac{5}{8}, \frac{7}{8}, \frac{8}{8}$

In *duple meter* there are two real beats in each measure, in *triple meter* there are three, in *quadruple meter* there are four, and in *quintuple meter* there are five.

In *simple meter* the unit regularly divides (or is divisible) into two divisions. Simple time signatures will use 2, 3, 4, or possibly 5 as their upper numbers, and a number representing a type of note as their lower number. In simple meters, for tempos between Andante and Allegro, the number of beats in the measure is given by the upper number and the type of note which receives the duration of one beat is shown by the lower number. Example 7—i includes several simple time signatures.

Example 7—i $\qquad \frac{2}{4} \qquad \frac{3}{8} \qquad \frac{4}{16} \qquad \frac{3}{4} \qquad \frac{4}{4} \qquad \frac{5}{4}$

The following unit, division, and sub-division patterns are those which occur in any simple meter which uses the quarter-note as the unit ($\frac{2}{4}, \frac{3}{4}, \frac{4}{4}$).

Example 7—j

Observe in example 7—j, pattern No. 9, which is called a *triplet*, and is an exception to the regular division into two pulsations which results in simple time. It may be thought of as being "borrowed" from compound time. Triplet patterns are possible in a wide variety of note values including those smaller than divisions, and those larger than units, as in example 7—k.

Example 7—k

In any meter wherein the half-note is the unit ($\mathbb{C}$, $\frac{2}{2}$, $\frac{3}{2}$, etc.) each note in example 7—j would be notated in note values double those given. In any meter wherein the eighth-note is the unit

$(\frac{2}{8}, \frac{3}{8}, \frac{4}{8},$ etc.,) the notes would be notated in note values half those given, but the proportional relationships remain constant.

In modern notation, the **C** has come to mean $\frac{4}{4}$ meter, or, occasionally $\frac{4}{2}$. The **¢** , alla breve, has come to mean $\frac{2}{2}$.[1]

In *compound meter* the unit regularly divides or is divisible into *three* divisions. Compound time signatures will use 6, 9, or 12 as their upper number, and a number representing a type of note as their lower number. The unit in compound time is always a dotted note or its equivalent. In compound meters, the number of actual beats in the measure is found by dividing the upper number by three. The type of note which receives one beat will be the sum of three of the type of note represented by the lower number. The lower number, therefore, represents the division (not the unit). Example 7—1 includes several compound time signatures.

Example 7—1 $\frac{6}{8}$ $\frac{9}{8}$ $\frac{12}{8}$ $\frac{6}{4}$ $\frac{9}{4}$ $\frac{12}{4}$

The unit, division, and sub-division patterns in example 7—m are the most frequently used in any compound meter which uses the dotted quarter note as the unit $(\frac{6}{8}, \frac{9}{8}, \frac{12}{8})$. In any meter wherein the dotted half-note is the unit $(\frac{6}{4}, \frac{9}{4}, \frac{12}{4})$ each note in example 7—m would be notated in note values double those given, and in any meter wherein the dotted eighth-note is the unit $(\frac{9}{16}, \frac{12}{16}, \frac{6}{16})$ the notes would be notated half those given, but the proportional relationships would remain constant.

Example 7—m

[1] During the thirteenth, fourteenth, and fifteenth centuries the symbols, **O** and **C** , were used as time signatures. The circle **O** was considered to be perfect, having no beginning and no end. It represented the Holy Trinity, and was used to show triple meter. The broken circle **C** represented imperfection and was used to show duple meter. The "alla breve," **¢** , was used to show that the long note should be performed at the shorter note's usual rate of speed.

Pattern No. 17 in example 7—m may also be written ♩. ♩. . In either notation it may be thought of as an exception, borrowed from simple time.

The division and sub-division patterns illustrated in this chapter are those used in instrumental notation. Vocal notation usually uses a separate eighth (or sixteenth-note, etc.) for each syllable of the text, connecting division and sub-division values only on melismas (one syllable of text with many notes).

Mixed meters are meters in which at least one unit beat is compound and at least one unit beat is simple, the division values being equal. Example 7—n includes several mixed meters.[2]

Example 7—n

Example 7—o shows the classification, unit, division, sub-division, conductor's beat pattern, and sample measures for several meters.

Example 7—o

Signatures	Number of beats in a measure	Classification	Unit	Division	Sub-division	Conductor's Beat Pattern	SAMPLE REPRESENTATIVE MEASURES
$\frac{6}{8}$	2	DC	♩.	♪	♪		
$\frac{9}{4}$	3	TC	♩.	♩	♪		
$\frac{12}{16}$	4	QC	♪	♪	♪		
$\frac{4}{4}$	4	QS	♩	♪	♪		
$\frac{2}{4}$	2	DS	♩	♪	♪		

_____

[2] Mixed meters are more thoroughly discussed in *Part II* of this book.

More sample measures can be found in Appendix III, Supplemental Rhythmic Exercises.

The following are conductor's beat patterns for compound meters having very slow tempos.

Example 7–p

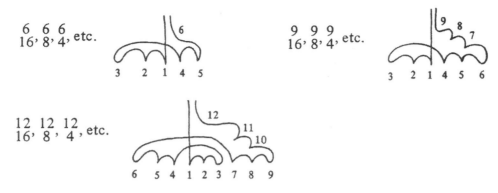

When the tempo for $\frac{5}{4}$ and $\frac{7}{4}$ is such that the quarter-note is the unit, $\frac{5}{4}$ is quintuple simple, and $\frac{7}{4}$ is septuple simple. The conductor's beat pattern for these meters is dependent on the placement of the secondary accents.

Example 7–q

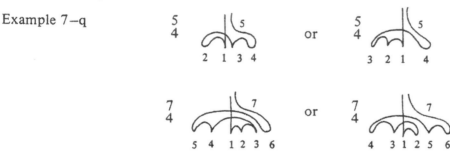

In the conductor's beat pattern, the primary accent, the first beat of the measure, is shown with a down beat. The secondary accent is shown by the horizontal motion across the body.

The *fermata* (⌢) is used over notes or rests which are to be prolonged. However, when *fermate* are found in seventeenth and eighteenth century chorales, they often indicate only the end of a line of the text and are not intended to be held longer than their value.

The term *"syncopation"* denotes the effect produced by the occurrence of an accent on a beat or portion of a beat where an accent is unexpected or unusual in that meter. An accent placed on a weak beat creates a syncopation. A tie between a short note and a longer note which falls on a beat also creates a syncopation. Example 7–r illustrates these two ways in which a syncopation may occur.

Example 7–r

Hemiola is a rhythmic device in which two triple simple measures are accented so as to create the effect of one triple simple measure having a unit double the value of the original unit. The hemiola figure typically has a duration of one or two measures before the rhythm returns to the original. The hemiola is generally notated without a meter change.

Example 7–s

The hemiola pattern in example 7–s results in an effect which could be written with a meter change as shown in example 7–t.

Example 7–t

Changing the meter from duple compound to triple simple, the divisions being constant, produces an effect similar to hemiola.[3]

Example 7–u

Keyboard Assignment 7

There is no specific *keyboard* assignment for this chapter, but a general lab assignment would include:

a.   Perform, by tapping the unit beat with one or both feet and tapping the notes with one hand (or sounding orally on a neutral syllable) Appendix III, Section I.

b.   Perform, in the manner described above, Appendix III, Section II.

c.   Perform, 'in the manner described above, Appendix III, Section III.

---

[3] Changing meters are more thoroughly discussed in *Part II* of this book.

CHAPTER 8
Triads

A *triad* is a group of three notes which can be arranged so that the interval of a third occurs between adjacent members of the chord. The components of a triad are its root, third, and fifth.

Example 8—a

fifth
third
root

A triad is named by references to its root and type. In a *major triad* the interval from the root to the third is a major third and the interval from the root to the fifth is a perfect fifth.

Example 8—b

G major triad
symbol: G (upper case denotes major)

In a *minor triad* the interval from the root to the third is a minor third and the interval from the root to the fifth is a perfect fifth.

Example 8—c

D minor triad
symbol:d (lower case denotes minor)

In an *augmented triad* the distance from the root to the third is a major third and the distance from the root to the fifth is an augmented fifth. (In the augmented triad, a major third occurs between the root and the third and between the third and the fifth.)

Example 8—d

F augmented triad
symbol: F⁺ (upper case with plus denotes augmented)

In a *diminished triad* the interval from the root to the third is a minor third and the interval from the root to the fifth is a diminished fifth. (In the diminished triad, a minor third occurs between the root and the third and between the third and the fifth.)

Example 8—e

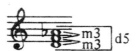

D diminished triad
symbol: d° (lower case with degree sign denotes diminished)

A major triad uses the first, third, and fifth steps of a major scale of the same name.

Example 8–f

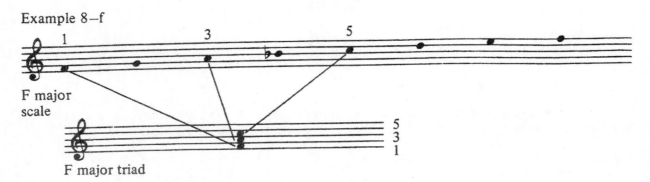

F major scale

F major triad

A minor triad uses the first, third, and fifth steps of a minor scale of the same name.

Example 8–g

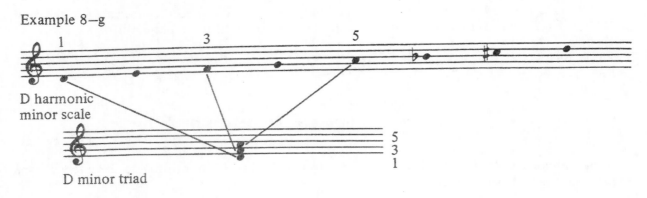

D harmonic minor scale

D minor triad

The *basic triads*, which occur on the staff when no sharps or flats are present, are shown in example 8–h.

Example 8–h

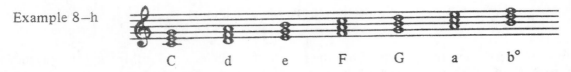

C   d   e   F   G   a   b°

A basic triad which is major remains major when each triad member is raised or lowered equally.

Example 8–i

G   Gb   G♯

A basic triad which is minor remains minor when each triad member is raised or lowered equally.

Example 8–j

d   d♯   db

The basic triad which is diminished remains diminished when each triad member is raised or lowered equally.

Example 8–k

A major triad may be made minor by lowering the third or by raising the root and fifth.

Example 8–l

A major triad may be made augmented by raising the fifth or by lowering the root and third.

Example 8–m

A minor triad may be made major by raising the third or by lowering the root and fifth.

Example 8–n

A minor triad may be made diminished by lowering the fifth or by raising the root and third.

Example 8–o

Keyboard Assignment 8

a. Play and spell any major or any augmented triad, with any given note as the root, third, or fifth.

b. Play and spell any minor or any diminished triad, with any given note as the root, third, or fifth.

CHAPTER 9

The Inversion of Triads, Figured Bass

Triads are in *root position* when the root of the chord sounds in the lowest voice. In *first inversion*, the third of the triad is in the lowest voice, and in *second inversion* the fifth is in the lowest voice.

Example 9—a

root   third   fifth

root position   first inversion   second inversion

Figured bass is a system of musical shorthand which became a common practice in the seventeenth century. Figured bass was a way in which a composer could denote the desired chords and inversions to be played in an accompaniment without writing out each note. The figures (numbers and/or accidentals) written below the bass note indicates intervals above the bass which are to be sounded. Figured bass does not indicate which specific chord member is in any particular upper voice. (Later, harmony teachers adopted figured bass symbols as a method of teaching seventeenth and eighteenth century harmonic practices.)

In figured bass notation, a bass note with no figure present is assumed to be the root of a triad.

Example 9—b

may be *realized*

If no figure is present, but an accidental is found below the bass note, that accidental is to be applied to the *third above* the bass.

Example 9—c

may be realized

The following symbols may be used to denote a triad in *root position*. Observe that, in each case, the third and fifth of the triad are assumed to be present in the chord, although the numbers 3 and 5 might not appear in the figured bass.

Example 9—d

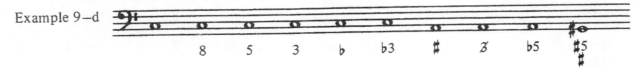

A *first inversion* triad is indicated by writing the number 6 under the bass note.

Example 9—e

realized

The interval of a third above the bass, which is also present in first inversion triads, is *assumed* and is not shown in the figured bass unless the third is to be altered. The altered third above the bass is indicated by the use of the appropriate accidental.

Example 9—f  realized

Second inversion triads are indicated by the figure $\frac{6}{4}$.

Example 9—g  realized

Accidentals in figured basses may be indicated by:

1. Placing an accidental in front of a number; the accidental is to be applied to that interval above the bass.

2. Placing an accidental by itself under a bass note; the accidental is to be applied only to the third above the bass.

3. A number with a diagonal line drawn through it, the interval represented by the number is to be raised a half-step.

Example 9—h 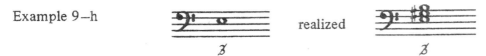 realized

Sometimes in actual eighteenth century scores which employ figured bass symbols, a flat is found indicating that a sharped note is to be lowered a half-step and a sharp is used to indicate that a flatted note is to be raised a half-step.

Example 9—i

Example 9—j

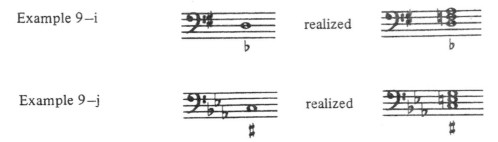

This text book, however, will follow the principle that whatever accidental is required in the music will be used in the figured bass analysis. Thus, a sharp used as in example 9—k is a precautionary accidental and will not result in a double sharp.

Example 9—k  realized

When a double sharp is required, in this text book, it will be indicated as follows.

Example 9–1 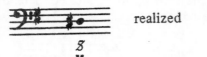 realized

Keyboard Assignment 9

Play, in three voices, any given major, minor, diminished, or augmented triad in root position, first inversion, or second inversion.

Example: Play a b♭ diminished triad in first inversion.   Answer:

CHAPTER 10
Triads Within Tonality

Tonality may be defined as the supremacy of one particular tone which lies at the center of a harmonic or melodic texture. Harmonically, strong tonality in Baroque and Classic literature results from the resolution of triad roots (frequently but not always) down by fifths toward the tonic triad and the frequent use of the tonic triad. Melodically, tonality is enhanced by the resolution of the *tendency tones* of the major scale and of the melodic and harmonic minor scales.

A *primary tendency* is a strong attraction between scale degrees. The second, fourth, and sixth scale degrees have a strong tendency to resolve into the first, third, and fifth scale degrees, respectively, and the seventh scale degree has a strong tendency to resolve upward to the eighth scale degree.

A *secondary tendency* is a weak attraction between scale degrees. Primary and secondary tendencies are illustrated in example 10—a.

Example 10—a

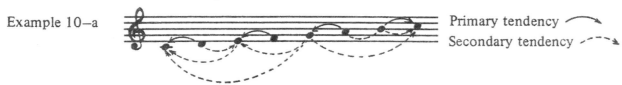

Primary tendency

Secondary tendency

Only a small number of melodies would be possible if composers resolved all tendency tones immediately. The immense variety of melodies found in music literature has resulted from the composer's prerogative to delay resolution of some tendency tones and to avoid resolution of other tendency tones. Example 10—b illustrates both immediate and delayed resolution of primary and secondary tendency tones.

Example 10—b

Symphony in B Minor   (delayed)   Schubert

The word *"diatonic"* means moving by step or half-step. When the term is applied to triads, diatonic denotes those triads which are drawn from a scale. The diatonic triads which occur in major tonality are of the following names and types (illustrated in D major).

Example 10—c

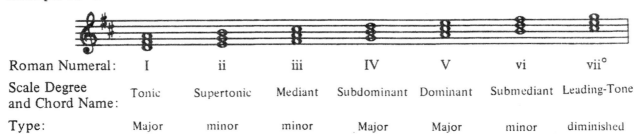

Roman Numeral:	I	ii	iii	IV	V	vi	vii°
Scale Degree and Chord Name:	Tonic	Supertonic	Mediant	Subdominant	Dominant	Submediant	Leading-Tone
Type:	Major	minor	minor	Major	Major	minor	diminished

33

The dominant is a perfect fifth above the tonic, the sub-dominant is a perfect fifth below the tonic. The *mediant* is the diatonic third between the tonic and the dominant; the sub-mediant is a diatonic third between the tonic and the sub-dominant below the tonic.

The diatonic triads which occur in harmonic minor tonality are of the following types (illustrated in D minor).

Example 10–d

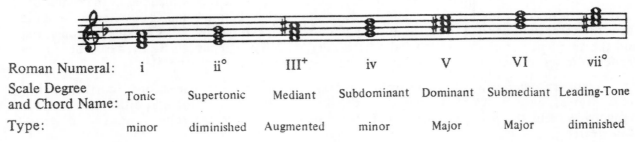

Roman Numeral:	i	ii°	III⁺	iv	V	VI	vii°
Scale Degree and Chord Name:	Tonic	Supertonic	Mediant	Subdominant	Dominant	Submediant	Leading-Tone
Type:	minor	diminished	Augmented	minor	Major	Major	diminished

In this book, when figured bass symbols are written *together* with Roman numerals, the figured bass accidentals are not shown. Thus in D Minor, the leading tone triad (C♯ E G) in first inversion will be analyzed: vii°₆, not vii°₆♯.

Keyboard Assignment 10

a. Play any specific triad in any major or harmonic minor key, in root position. Example: Play the dominant in C♯ minor. Solution:

b. Sing, using letters, the triads in the chord series (progression) tonic, subdominant, dominant, tonic in major and minor keys of up to and including two sharps and two flats. The following example is illustrated in D minor.

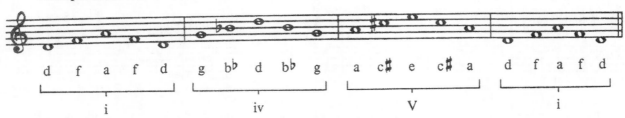

d f a f d	g b♭ d b♭ g	a c♯ e c♯ a	d f a f d
i	iv	V	i

34

CHAPTER 11

The Major-Minor Seventh Chord, Non-Harmonic Tones in Analysis

An additional tone, the seventh, may be added to any triad. This tone is a seventh above the triad's root, and a third above the triad's fifth.

Example 11—a

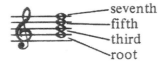

The seventh chord most frequently found in eighteenth and nineteenth century literature is that which is comprised of a major triad with a minor seventh added above the root. Because of its construction, the chord is designated *"major-minor seventh chord,"* or Mm7. (In contemporary commercial music, the chord illustrated in example 11—a is called "G7.")

The most frequent occurrence of this chord is its use as a diatonic seventh chord on the fifth scale degree, the dominant, in both major and minor keys. In such circumstances, the chord is appropriately designated the *"dominant seventh chord."*

When a dominant seventh chord is used in root position, the figured bass symbol in major keys is 7. When used in minor keys, the figured bass symbol is $\frac{7}{\natural}$.

Example 11—b

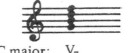

When used in first inversion, the figured bass symbol is $\frac{6}{5}$. When used in second inversion, the figured bass symbol is $\frac{4}{3}$ and when used in third inversion, the figured bass symbol is $\frac{4}{2}$. See example 11—c.

Example 11—c

Non-harmonic tones are those tones in a musical texture which are not chord members. Non-harmonic tones are classified by their manner of approach and their manner of resolution. A detailed discussion of non-harmonic tones appears in Chapter 22. However, there are four types of non-harmonic tones which are introduced here. Their recognition will enhance the students' perception of the musical examples.

The *passing tone* (P.T.) is a non-harmonic tone which is approached and resolved by a step or half-step (scalewise), continuing in the same direction. When a passing tone falls on a stronger beat or portion beat than its resolution, it is an *accented passing tone.*

Example 11–d Passing Tone   Accented P.T.

The *neighboring tone* (N.T.) is a non-harmonic tone which is approached scalewise and resolves scalewise opposite to the approach. Neighboring tones may also be accented.

Example 11–e Neighboring Tone   Accented N.T.

 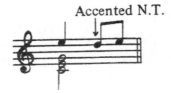

The *suspension (sus.)* is a non-harmonic tone which is approached by preparation—by sounding in the same voice immediately prior to becoming a non-harmonic tone. The suspension resolves down scalewise. "Suspensions" which resolve upward are generally designated *retardations*.

Example 11–f Suspension   Retardation

The *appoggiatura* (appogg.) is a non-harmonic tone which is approached by a leap and resolved scalewise.

Example 11–g   Appoggiatura

Keyboard Assignment 11

Play the dominant seventh chord of any major or minor key in root position or in any inversion.

CHAPTER 12

The Baroque

The *Baroque* period of music history is generally considered to begin about 1600, with the birth of opera, and to close about 1750 with the death of J. S. Bach and the advent of a new style. The forms of particular importance in the Baroque period were the opera, oratorio, cantata, chorale, suite, toccata, sonata, variation, prelude and fugue, chorale prelude, passacaglia, chaconne, and concerto grosso. The composers of greatest stature were Monteverdi, Andrea and Giovanni Gabrieli, Schütz, Buxtehude, Vivaldi, J. S. Bach, Handel, Telemann, and Domenico and Allesandro Scarlatti.

The term Baroque was probably derived from the Portuguese word *Barrôco,* meaning a pearl of irregular shape. The term was applied originally by critics who felt that this highly polyphonic and often bombastic music was so ornate as to be grotesque.

The following compositions are representative of the Baroque Period's two greatest composers, Bach and Handel.

Example 12–a

French Suite in G, Bach. In Germany during the early part of the eighteenth century, the suite generally consisted of a series of short dance movements, all in the same key. The movements almost inevitably present in the suite were the *Allemande* (a "German" dance in a moderate tempo in quadruple simple meter), the *Courante* (a "running" dance in a quick triple simple meter), the *Sarabande* (a moderately slow dance in triple simple meter), and the *Gigue* (a fast movement in duple, triple, or quadruple compound meter). Between the Sarabande and the Gigue, other "optional" dances frequently appear; in this suite, Bach has added a Gavotte, a Bourée and a Loure.

(On the next page)

SUITE V.

G major

Bach

ALLEMANDE

COURANTE.

SARABANDE.

GAVOTTE.

Allegro ♩=80.

BOURRÉE.

Allegro. ♩=96.

LOURE. [4]

Moderato. ♩ = 180.

43

GIGUE.

44

Example 12–b

Concerto Grosso, Op. 6, No. 1, Handel. The Concerto Grosso is an instrumental composition in which a small group is featured prominently against and contrasted to, the larger ensemble, which is generally a string orchestra. The solo group, *"concertino,"* in this concerto consists of the first Violin I and II and the cello. The larger ensemble, *"ripieno,"* consists of the second Violin I and II, the viola, and the basso continuo.

Concerto I

Handel

46

47

48

49

50

51

54

55

56

57

58

Example 12–c

Chorale, *Cantata Sinfonia,* and *First Movement: "Christ lag in Todesbanden,"* Bach. The German title of this chorale translates: *"Christ Lay in the Bonds of Death."* Almost all of the approximately 300 cantatas that Bach wrote are based, as is this cantata, upon a chorale melody.

Chorale: *"Christ lag in Todesbanden"*   Bach[1]

---

[1] The "Bach Chorales" are harmonizations, made by J. S. Bach, of melodies from many sources. Many chorale melodies pre-date Bach by two centuries.

Cantata, *Christ lag in Todesbanden*   Bach

SINFONIA.

63

60

sein,   Hal - le - - lu-jah,hal-le - lu -   jah,   hal-le - lu-

sein und sin - gen   Hal -   le - lu -   jah, hal-le - - lu -jah,

sein,   Hal-le - - lu-jah,hal-le-,hal-le-lu - jah,   und   sin - gen

jah,   hal-le-,hal-le-lu - jah,   und sin - gen   hal - - le - lu -

hal-le-lu-jah,hal-le-lu -   jah,   hal-le - - lu -   jah,   hal-le-,hal-le-lu-

hal - - le - lu - jah,hal-le - - lu-jah,   hal-le-lu-jah,hal-le-lu-

73

Alla breve

74

70

(There is no specific keyboard assignment for this chapter.)

78

CHAPTER 13

Major and Minor Triads in Four-Part Harmony

The composers of the Baroque, and to a considerable extent, the composers of the following periods, showed a preference for writing in four independent voices, or parts, both in choral and instrumental compositions.

In choral writing, the following *ranges* have generally been observed by composers. Notes which are found only occasionally and which may be considered extreme are shown in parentheses.

Example 13–a

Composers generally arrange voices in *order* from high to low: Soprano, alto, tenor, bass. Occasionally, however, lines are found to be out of their customary order due to the melodic curve evolving in one or more of the parts. In example 13–b, the tenor line crosses over the alto at two points.

Example 13–b

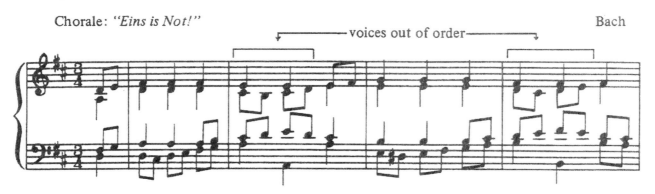

The distance between the soprano and alto and between the alto and tenor is seldom greater than an octave in Baroque four-part writing. This practice was occasionally disregarded, apparently to enhance a melodic line. The distance between the bass and tenor is frequently greater than an octave.

Example 13–c

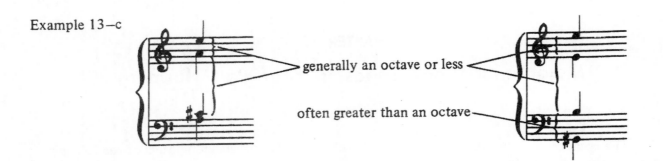

generally an octave or less

often greater than an octave

Chords are in *close structure* when an octave or less occurs between the *soprano* and the *tenor*.

Example 13–d

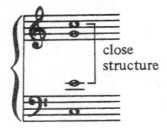

close structure

Chords are in *open structure* when the distance between the *soprano* and *tenor exceeds an octave*.

Example 13–e

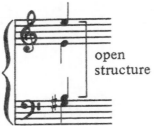

open structure

In the writing of major and minor triads in root position in four voices, composers have consistently doubled the root. (Exceptions to this principle again involve melodic lines in individual parts, and will be discussed in detail in Chapter 14.)

Keyboard Assignment 13

Following typical Baroque practice relative to distance between voices, doublings, etc.:

a. Play the following triads in four-part harmony in close structure, with the root in the soprano. (Check distance between voices, and doubling.)

    eb min.   B Maj.   Ab Maj.   c# min.   f# min.   g min.   Bb Maj.

b. Play the triads in a. above, in open structure, with the third in the soprano.

c. Play these isolated figured bass problems at the keyboard with the fifth in the soprano, in open structure. Identify the triad.

80

CHAPTER 14

Connecting Major and Minor Triads in Root Position in Major Keys

Composers of every style period have found it necessary to combine simultaneously sounding *melodic lines* in the individual parts in such a way as to produce *harmonic structure* that they consider suitable. A composer's harmonic style depends largely upon how he or she chooses to reconcile the requirements of the vertical sonorities and the horizontal lines in a musical texture. The Baroque composers were fairly consistent in their treatment of certain basic partwriting situations, and from these consistencies, the following principles may be drawn.

1. *Move to the nearest chord tone.* In connecting two chords, any voice may move either up or down to the nearest available chord tone that will result in the strongest possible vertical sonority.

Example 14—a

G: I   ii

2. *Keep the common tone.* In instances where two chords have one or more notes in common, this note is generally retained in the same voice.

Example 14—b

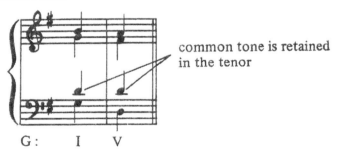

common tone is retained in the tenor

G: I   V

3. *Maintain voice independence.* Baroque composers were consistent in maintaining independence between the voices in a musical texture. Two voices moving together in a parallel unison, parallel octave, or parallel perfect fifth cause a temporary loss in voice independence. This effect is outside the style.

Example 14—c—1   Example 14—c—2   Example 14—c—3

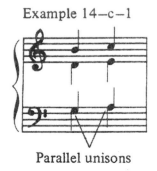      

Parallel unisons   Parallel fifths   Parallel octaves

The same two voices must be involved in the parallel fifth or octave relationship for any uncharacteristic parallelism to exist. Parallel fifths and octaves are also outside the style when they are *compound intervals* (larger than an octave).

An octave doubling as reinforcement of an independent voice such as occurs in keyboard and instrumental music does not cause a temporary loss of independence between independent voices, and is therefore within the Baroque and subsequent styles.

The Baroque composers did not write parallel octaves or parallel fifths by contrary motion, as shown in example 14–d.

Example 14–d

(The effect illustrated in example 14–d–2 and example 14–d–3 is often found as the final chords of compositions by composers writing thirty to fifty years after the close of the Baroque period—see Beethoven's Sonata, Op. 10, No. 1, conclusion of First Movement.)

A diminished fifth may move to a perfect fifth in four-part Baroque style.

Example 14–e

Chorale: *"Aus meines Herzens Grunde"*   Bach

Baroque composers used the principle of *contrary motion* to maintain the independence of the parts, especially when connecting root position triads with roots a second apart. Contrary motion is especially characteristic between those voices having a fifth or octave relationship, as in example 14–f and 14–g.

82

Example 14–f

Chorale: *"Du Lebensfürst, Herr Jesu Christ"*   Bach

G: I   vi   V   I   I₆

Example 14–g

Chorale: *"Nun lob, mein Seel, den Herren"*   Bach

A: I   vi   iii   IV

Contrary motion between voices having an octave or Perfect fifth relationship is especially characteristic when the soprano and bass parts move in parallel tenths, as in example 14–h.

Example 14–h

Chorale: *"O Ewigkeit, du Donnerwort"*   Bach

F: I   I   vii°₆   I₆

4. *Change of structure.* A change of structure within a phrase often results in parallel fifths or parallel octaves, or in uncharacteristically large leaps in one or more of the voices. There are, however, points at which structure may be changed within the style. These points are:

a. Structure may be changed (large leaps may occur) where a chord is repeated. In addition, structure may change by adjusting inner voices while holding the soprano and bass. Occasionally, in this kind of circumstance, Baroque composers interpolated a chord tone between two otherwise uncharacteristic perfect intervals.

83

Example 14—i

Chorale: *"Wo soll ich fliehen hin"*   Bach

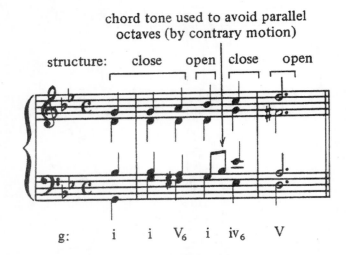

b. Structure may be changed at a point of irregular voice leading, often implemented by retaining the common tone and moving the tenor a fourth. Baroque composers often employed this procedure in the progression V—I, especially at phrase endings.

Example 14—j

Chorale: *"Werde munter, mein Gemüte"*   Bach

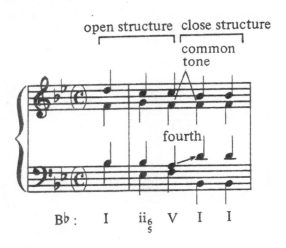

c. At a point of irregular doubling, it is sometimes advantageous to change structure. Example 14—k—1 changes structure after the irregularly doubled supertonic chord, with characteristically smooth part-writing in the alto and tenor parts. Example 14—k—2 maintains close structure throughout the example, but parallel fifths by contrary motion result between the bass and alto voices and the tenor moves an augmented fourth. The augmented fourth interval is not used this way in Baroque four-voice style.

84

Example 14—k

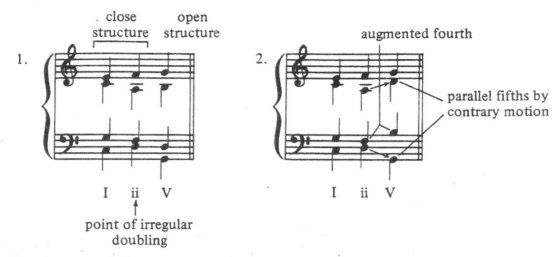

5. *The augmented fourth.* The augmented fourth as found in the tenor voice in example 14—k—2 was consistently avoided by Baroque composers. When used melodically between two different chords, the augmented fourth is out of the style. The diminished fifth, however, is found occuring melodically within the Baroque style, as illustrated by the final two chords in the tenor voice in example 14—i. The augmented fourth occurs melodically in the Baroque style when both tones are chord members of a continuing sonority. The augmented fourth in example 14—l occurs as both B and F are members of the major-minor seventh chord on G.

Example 14—l

Concerto in D Minor for Two Violins   Bach
Second Movement, Measures 38 and 39

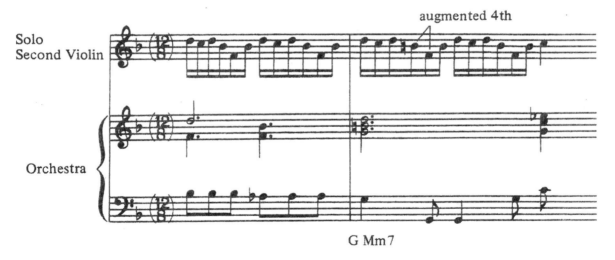

6. *The leading-tone.* Baroque composers, and composers of subsequent periods, were fairly consistent in avoiding doubling the leading-tone. Rare exceptions to this principle involve strong melodic lines moving in contrary motion through the leading tone. An example of this occurs in example 13—b, in the second complete measure. The leading-tone has a strong tendency to resolve up scalewise when it occurs in the soprano or bass part, and the harmony is V or vii°. However, in the Bach chorales, a majority of the leading-tones found in inner voices at phrase endings (cadences) resolve down by a third, a practice which allows the final chord to be complete.

Example 14-m

Chorale: *"Ermuntre dich, mein schwacher Geist"*   Bach

Leading tone resolved
down a third

G: V⁴₂   I   V   I

Questions Frequently Asked

Question: Why is it important that students learn four-voice partwriting technique?

Answer: There has been, in this century, a great increase in the amount of information that students are expected to learn, and, in view of that fact, the question is reasonable.

1. The four-voice, quasi-chorale structure appears in choral, brass, and string compositions in which the student will be performing, or which the student will eventually be conducting. A thorough knowledge of a style allows the music to be learned more rapidly and securely, and to be performed with greater sensitivity.

2. Much instrumental music, whether keyboard, orchestral, or wind ensemble, is essentially a four-voice texture. The four-voice style can represent a wide range of textures, condensed and consolidated for purposes of harmonic analysis.

3. The four-voice texture is a convenient way to show chord spellings, and preparation and resolution of dissonances and tendency tones, without having the student spend time writing sonatas and concertos to illustrate each technique being examined.

4. The student working in four-voice technique has an opportunity to learn how composers of all style-periods have worked to achieve a balance between the horizontal elements of music (melody and counterpoint) and the vertical element of music (harmony). Basic technique, or skill, in achieving this balance can transfer to other musical styles.

5. The four-voice technique allows all students access to the material regardless of their keyboard skills, whereas theory courses based on sonatas and symphonies, at this stage, would exclude a majority of the students. This easy-access to the four-voice material helps the student to develop aural skills. The student *must* play at a keyboard everything that he or she has written, both as an aid to understanding the material, but also, perhaps even more important, as a key element in ear-training development. After playing what he or she has written, the student should practice looking at the progressions, imagining the sounds occurring in his or her mind. This is the inner game of ear-training. Over time, the student can develop a large "repertoire" of progressions that he or she can recognize.

Question: To what extent do the principles discussed in this book, which concentrates on the eighteenth century, apply to other style periods?

Answer: From the middle of the seventeenth century through the nineteenth century the musical "vocabulary" was so universal that this period of music history is referred to as the "Common Practice Period." There are, of course, stylistic differences—Bach does not sound like Chopin, but these differences are the result of different applications of the same material. The differences between Baroque (seventeeth through half of the eighteenth century), Classic (second half of the eighteenth century) and Romantic (nineteenth century) music are not a matter of basic harmonic vocabulary, but are, instead, a result of different textures, forms, and instrumentation.

Keyboard Assignment 14

Play the following progressions in four parts in all major keys, around the circle of fifths.

(Instructional note: In assignments of this type, students are to use no written aids other than the progressions as written in the original key.)

87

CHAPTER 15

Harmonic Minor, Connecting Major and Minor Triads in Root Position

The *harmonic minor* scale is derived from the consistent treatment of scale degrees by Baroque and later composers. The tones found in the harmonic minor scale are those normally used in the Baroque style.

The triad types which are derived from the harmonic minor scale are shown in example 15–a.

Example 15–a

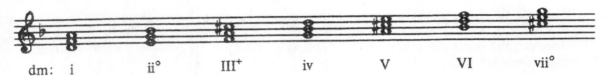

dm: i   ii°   III⁺   iv   V   VI   vii°

When connecting two different triads, Baroque composers avoided moving a voice an augmented second, the interval which occurs between the sixth and seventh scale degrees in the harmonic minor scale.

Example 15–b

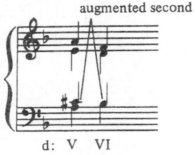

d: V   VI

The augmented second was avoided under the circumstances illustrated in example 15–b, probably because performers found the interval difficult to perform in tune (except, of course, on keyboard instruments).

The augmented second was avoided in either one of two ways, 1) by using either the raised or lowered tones of the melodic minor scale (discussed in Chapter 17), or by 2) using irregular doubling. Irregular doubling is typically employed in the progression V–VI in harmonic minor writing.

Example 15–c

Chorale: *"Christ lag in Todesbanden"*   Bach

doubled third

d: V   VI

In the harmonic minor in the Baroque style, the augmented second in example 15—b would have been removed by doubling the third instead of the root in the sub-mediant triad.

Example 15—d

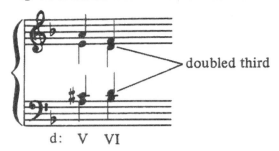

d:　V　VI

doubled third

Baroque (and subsequent) composers occasionally used the augmented second in a melodic line moving against a continuing dominant sonority ($V_{(7)}$ or $vii^{\circ}_{(7^{\circ})}$). This is especially true in keyboard music.

Example 15—e

Partita in C Minor, Sinfonia   Bach

augmented second

g:　V　　　　　　　i

Many Baroque compositions written in minor keys conclude with a major tonic triad, an effect known as the *Picardy Third*.

Example 15—f

Chorale: *"Erschienen ist der herrlich Tag"*   Bach

f♯:　　vii°₆　i₆₄　V₇　　I

Picardy third

Many examples from music literature are in a key that differs from the key of their signature, as in examples 15—c, 15—e, and 15—f. This occurs primarily for two reasons: 1) composers often move through related (differing by one accidental) keys, and sometimes move through unrelated

89

(differing by two or more accidentals) keys for tonal variety, and 2) the composer may be using the ascending form of melodic minor in much of a composition; the last flat of any minor key signature lowers the sixth scale degree and might therefore be omitted for convenience.

Question Frequently Asked

Question: The leading-tone seems to be a difficult note, with a confusing number of things it must do, or must not do. Will you summarize everything that students should know about the leading-tone?

Answer: The leading-tone was seldom doubled because of its strength as a tendency-tone. That parallel octaves result when the doubled leading-tone resolves is incorrect, because not all leading-tones resolve up, as shown below. The leading-tone has a strong tendency to resolve up when it appears in an outer voice and the harmony containing the leading-tone is dominant in function (V or vii°. However, the leading-tone may move down by half step in chromatic writing, and may move in other ways as required by the harmony. The following examples summarize the Common Practice Period treatment of the leading tone, in this case, the note B. (Class discussion: How do examples 10, 11, 12 and 13 illustrate the "give and take" between the horizontal and the vertical elements of music? Which element has been favored and which element has been compromised in each of those examples?)

Keyboard Assignment 15

Play the following progressions in all minor keys, around the circle of fifths.

a.

a: i   iv   V   i

b.

a: i   VI   iv   V   VI

CHAPTER 16

Triads in Inversion

By using inversions, a composer is often able to create bass lines which have greater melodic interest than is possible with exclusively root position triads. In addition, the use of inversions allows for a greater variety in the vertical sonorities.

Triads in First Inversion in Baroque four-voice style.

Major and *minor* triads in first inversion are typically found with the *soprano* tone doubled.

Example 16—a—1

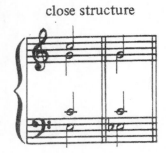   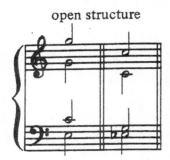

The first inversion major triad with the chord third in the soprano, though rare, is occasionally found as the bass and soprano move scalewise in contrary motion through an octave.

Example 16—a—2

Chorale: *"Aus meines Herzens Grunde"*   Bach

G: I   V₆   vi₆₅   vii°₆   I₆   ii₆₅   V   I

Minor triads are also frequently found with the third of the chord doubled.

Example 16—b

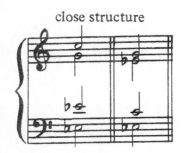   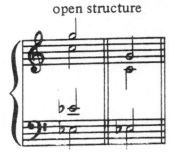

Diminished triads are typically used in first inversion with the third doubled.

Example 16–c

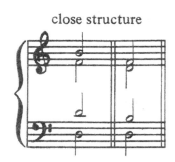
close structure

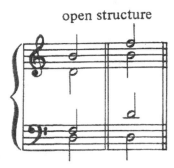
open structure

Diminished triads are seldom encountered in root position or in second inversion.

Augmented triads are so infrequently found as to be almost outside the Baroque style. The few augmented triads which do occur are usually used in first inversion with the third doubled. (The root position leading tone triad in example 16–d is a rare exception to the general usage of that chord.)

Example 16–d

Chorale: *"O Ewigkeit, du Donnerwort"*   Bach

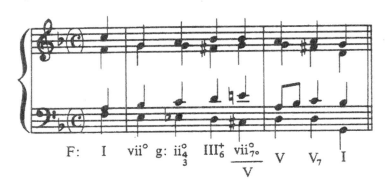

F: I   vii°   g: ii°$_4^3$ III$_6^+$ $\dfrac{\text{vii}°_{7°}}{\text{V}}$ V   V$_7$ I

The composers of the Baroque and subsequent periods frequently used *irregular doubling* where it enabled them to create more interesting horizontal lines in the individual parts. The doubling in the third chord of example 16–e is irregular, but it allows for the interesting line found in the tenor part.

Example 16–e

Chorale: *"Allein Gott in der Höh sei Erh"*   Bach

irregular doubling

G: I   I   IV$_6$ V   ii   vi   ii$_6$ V
                                    e: iv$_6$

93

Likewise, composers use irregular doubling to avoid a part-writing error. When two or more first inversions are used in a series, a composer will quite likely use irregular doublings to avoid parallel octaves. In example 16—f, the doublings are regular, but parallel octaves and fifths occur.

Example 16—f

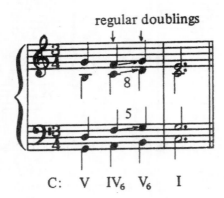

regular doublings

C: V   IV₆   V₆   I

In example 16—g, the same chords and inversions are used, but the parallel fifths and octaves are removed by the use of an irregular doubling.

Example 16—g

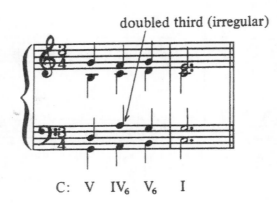

doubled third (irregular)

C: V   IV₆   V₆   I

Baroque composers often changed structure following a first inversion chord where such a change in structure resulted in lines having fewer leaps. Example 16—h—1 is more often encountered in the Baroque style than example 16—h—2; the former changes structure but has no leaps, whereas the latter maintains the structure but has two leaps.

Example 16—h   1.

F: I   V₆   I

2.

F: I   V₆   I

The mediant and sub-mediant triads are seldom used in first inversion in Baroque writings. When they do occur, the bass typically departs scalewise, as in example 16—i.

Example 16—i

Chorale: *"Aus meines Herzens Grunde"*   Bach

rare

G: vi   vi   iii$_6$ ii$_6$ I$_6$ V$_7$ I$_6$

Occasionally, inverted mediant and sub-mediant triads are used to effect a change of key. (See Chapter 20.)

Example 16—j

Chorale: *"Gott sei gelobet und gebenedeiet"*   Bach

(neighboring tone)

C: I   V$_6$ V   vi$_6$ V   vi   V$^4_3$ I$^6_4$ I

G: ii$_6$ V   V$_7$

Triads in Second Inversion in Baroque four-voice style.

Triads in second inversion are used considerably less than are triads in root position and first inversion. Second inversion triads are generally restricted to the following types.

The *cadential $\frac{6}{4}$ chord* is the most frequently found second inversion type. It involves the tonic triad used on an accented beat near the phrase ending (cadence, see Chapter 18). The chord is used with a doubled fifth and usually resolves to V. The cadential $\frac{6}{4}$ chord is generally approached from vi, IV$_{(6)}$, ii$_{(6)}$, or I$_{(6)}$.

Cadential $\frac{6}{4}$ chords are illustrated in example 16—k and 16—l. The octave relationship between the doubled fifth of the cadential $\frac{6}{4}$ chord and the doubled root of the dominant is in the style.

95

Example 16—k

Chorale: *"Das neugeborne Kindelein"*   Bach

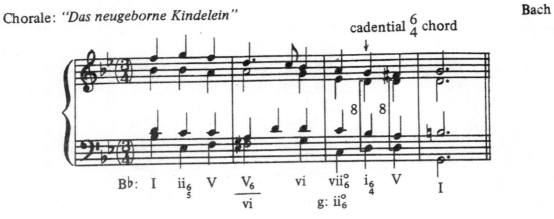

Bb: I   ii6/5 V   V6/vi   vi   vii°6 i6/4 V   I

g: ii°6

Example 16—1

Chorale: *"Lobt Gott, ihr Christen allzugleich"*   Bach

G: I   IV6 ii6/5 I6/4 V   I

The passing $\frac{6}{4}$ chord is a second inversion triad (usually the tonic) formed as voices, moving scalewise or retaining common tones, combine to form a chord with its fifth in the bass. The most frequently found passing $\frac{6}{4}$ chord is preceeded by IV6 and followed by ii6/5, as shown in example 16—m.

Example 16—m

Chorale: *"O Haupt voll Blut und Wurden"*   Bach

Eb: I   IV6 I6/4 ii6/5 V   I

The pedal $\frac{6}{4}$ chord almost invariably involves the use of a subdominant triad over a sustained tonic pedal, as in example 16–n.

Example 16–n

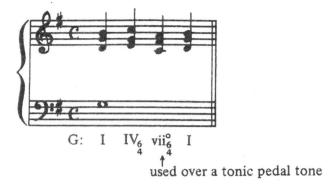

G: I IV_6^4 $vii°_6^4$ I

↑
used over a tonic pedal tone

The pedal $\frac{6}{4}$ is a frequently used device in keyboard music.

Example 16–o

Prelude XV, WTC Book I   Bach

pedal tone

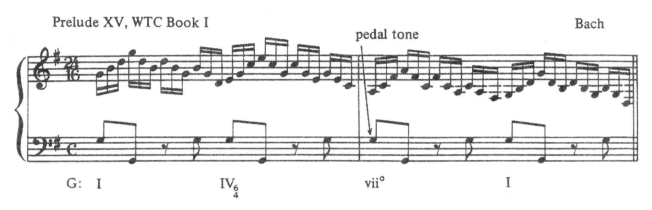

G: I IV_6^4 vii°   I

The arpeggio $\frac{6}{4}$ chord is a type of second inversion chord in which the bass both approaches and departs the fifth of a chord by leap. In this $\frac{6}{4}$ pattern, the chord of approach, the second inversion chord, and the chord of resolution are the same chord, in different positions.

Example 16–p

Minuet II, *French Suite in D Minor*   Bach

F: vi ii_7 V

↑   ↑
arpeggio   arpeggio
$\frac{6}{4}$ chord $\frac{6}{4}$ chord

97

Second inversion supertonic, mediant, submediant, and leading tone triads are seldom found in the Baroque style.

The use of inversions necessitates and justifies occasional leaps of fourths and fifths in the inner voices.

Keyboard Assignment 16

a. Play the following progressions around the circle of fifths in all major keys.

b. Play a—2 in all minor keys, around the circle of fifths.

CHAPTER 17

Melodic Minor

The *melodic minor* scale is a theoretical codification reflecting the treatment of the sixth and seventh scale degrees often found in minor keys in Baroque style. The harmonic minor scale has, between its sixth and seventh degrees, an augmented second, which eighteenth century composers avoided in certain circumstances, as discussed in Chapter 15. Augmented seconds were avoided by raising the sixth scale degree when it was associated with the raised seventh degree, and by lowering the seventh degree when it was associated with the lowered sixth degree. Frequently the sixth and seventh scale degrees were raised in ascending passages, and lowered in descending passages. The leading-tone (the raised seventh step) occurs at cadences, phrase endings (see Chapter 18), almost without exception.

Example 17—a

Italian Concerto, Third Movement

Bach

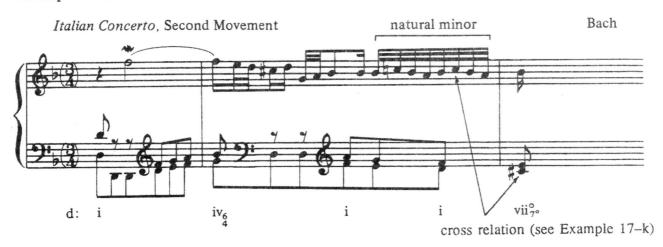

A melodic line may use the tones of natural minor (the descending form of melodic minor) both ascending or descending when the underlying harmony is the tonic, supertonic, subdominant, or submediant triad.

Example 17—b

Italian Concerto, Second Movement

Bach

99

A melodic line typically uses the tones of the ascending form of melodic minor both ascending and descending when the underlying harmony is the dominant.

Example 17–c

Minuet in G Minor

Bach

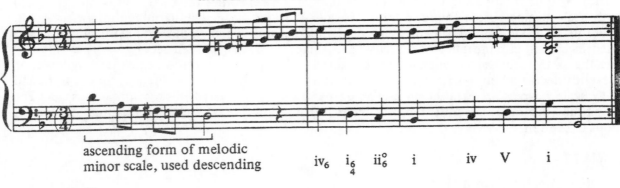

Baroque composers frequently wrote lines which descend chromatically through both the raised and lowered forms of the sixth and seventh degrees.

Example 17–d

Mass in B Minor, *Crucifixus*

Bach

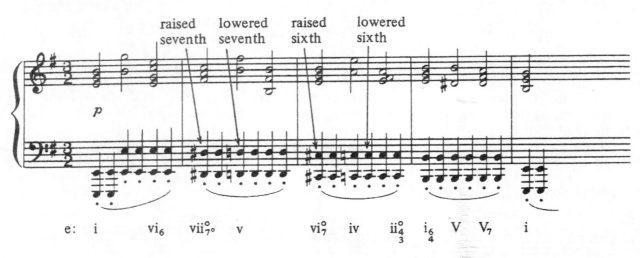

The use of the descending form of melodic minor may result in a minor dominant, as illustrated in example 17–e and 17–f.

Example 17—e

Chorale: *"Jesu, meine Freude"* Bach

e: i v₆ iv₆ vii°7°⁴₂ VI ii°⁶₅ V i

Example 17—f

Minuet in G Minor Bach

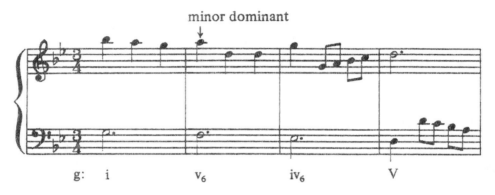

g: i v₆ iv₆ V

The descending form of melodic minor may result in a major mediant triad, as illustrated in example 17—g.

Example 17—g

Chorale: *"Jesu, meine Freude"* Bach

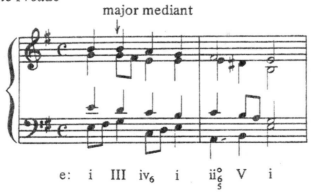

e: i III iv₆ i ii°⁶₅ V i

The use of the ascending form of melodic minor can result in a major triad or major-minor seventh chord on the sub-dominant. (The raised sixth step was not doubled on the accented portion of a beat.)

Example 17–h

Chorale: *"Jesu, meine Freude"*

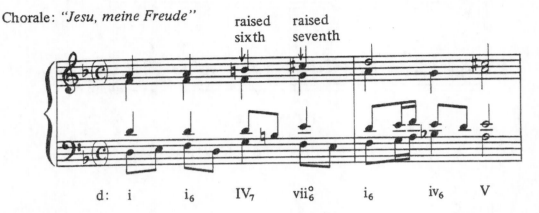

The tonic triad type is the same in both melodic minor and harmonic minor. All the other triad types are different. Example 17–i (although from a period some thirty years after the Baroque) illustrates the use of a major VII (sub-tonic) and a minor dominant.

Example 17–i

Piano Sonata, K. 332, Third Movement   Mozart (1778)

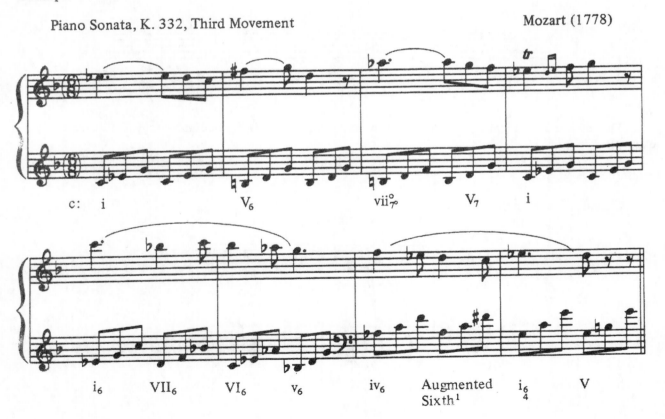

---

[1] Augmented sixth chords are altered chords discussed in detail in *Part II*, Chapter 5.

The tones in melodic minor writing which differ from those found in harmonic minor, namely the raised sixth and the lowered seventh, are the tones which the Baroque composers treated as special. These tones are not typically departed by leap, in diatonic harmony, but rather are nearly always associated with the adjacent tone in the melodic minor scale—the raised sixth step with the raised seventh and the lowered seventh step with the lowered sixth.

The following example summarizes the typical Baroque use of melodic minor.

Example 17–j

Chorale: *"O Mensch, schau Jesum Christum an"*

Bach

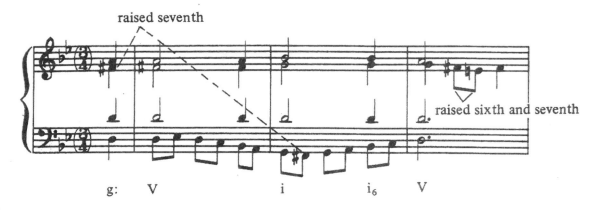

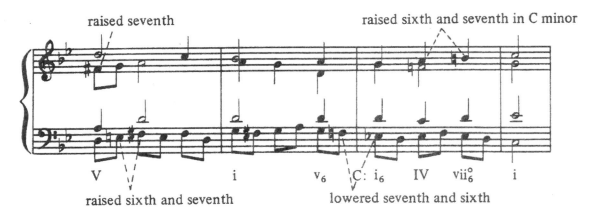

A cross relation is the use of chromatic forms of the same note, these forms differing by one half-step, and appearing in different voices in immediately adjacent harmonies.

Example 17–k

Cross relations are generally outside the Baroque style. However, cross relations involving the raised or lowered tones of the melodic minor scale are within the Baroque style, as illustrated in example 17—a, and 17—b. (Cross relations involving certain altered chords, specifically secondary dominants, are also found in the style.)

The raised sixth degree was not often doubled by Baroque writers, especially on a strong portion of a beat.

Keyboard Assignment 17

Play the following progressions around the circle of fifths in all minor keys.

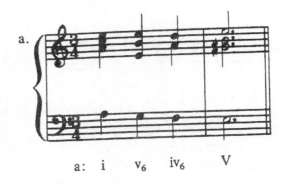

a: i v_6 iv_6 V

a: i   IV vii^o_6 i

CHAPTER 18

The Harmonic Cadences

A harmonic cadence is a progression which concludes a musical phrase. Composers have used a variety of cadential progressions for achieving clarity of form and varying degrees of finality at phrase endings.

The *perfect authentic* cadence is the strongest, or most final, of all harmonic cadence patterns. In this cadence, a root position dominant, or dominant seventh, moves to a root position tonic triad, with the root in the soprano voice of the final chord.

Example 18—a   1.

a: V   i

2.

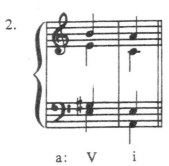

a: V   i

The *imperfect authentic* cadence results when the dominant—tonic progression appears at the cadence with the dominant in inversion, or with the tonic having its third or fifth in the soprano. The use of the leading tone triad moving to the tonic also results in an imperfect authentic cadence.

Example 18—b   1.

C: V   I

2.

C: V₆   I

3.

c: vii°₆ i

The *perfect plagal* cadence results when, at a phrase ending, a root position sub-dominant triad moves to a root position tonic triad with the root in the soprano of the final chord.

Example 18—c   1.

C: IV   I

2.

c: iv i

The *imperfect plagal* cadence results when the sub-dominant—tonic progression appears at the cadence with the sub-dominant in inversion, or with the tonic having its third or fifth in the soprano. The use of the supertonic triad or seventh chord (almost always in first inversion) also results in an imperfect plagal cadence.

Example 18—d

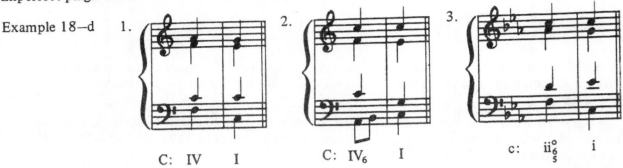

Plagal cadences allowed composers to harmonize a sustained tonic tone in the soprano voice, extending the end of a phrase.

Example 18—e

Chorale: *"Lob und Preis sei Gott dem Vater und dem Sohn"*   Bach

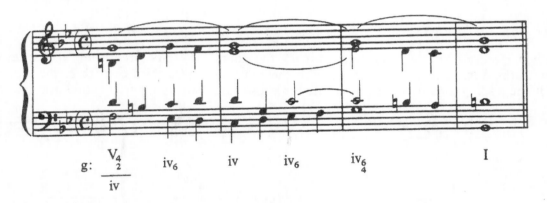

The *half cadence* results when a phrase ends on the dominant, dominant seventh, or on the leading tone triad, or, in rare instances, on the sub-dominant triad. The chord preceding the dominant is typically the tonic in any position, or the supertonic or sub-dominant in root position or first inversion. The half cadence in minor invariably uses the major dominant.

Example 18—f

Composers have used the half cadence to create phrases which have shape (form) but which flow fluently across the phrase ending. A "question—answer" effect between phrases is enhanced by the use of a half cadence.

Example 18–g

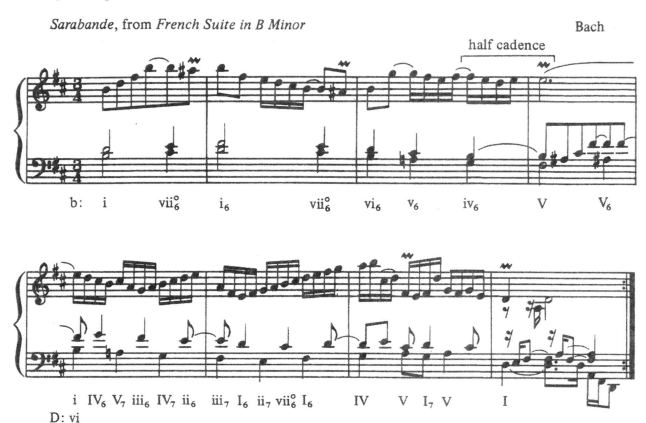

Sarabande, from *French Suite in B Minor*   Bach

The *phrygian cadence* is a form of half cadence, in which the fifth scale degree is approached scalewise in the two outer voices in contrary motion and is harmonized by the dominant. The phrygian cadence is found only in minor keys.

Example 18–h

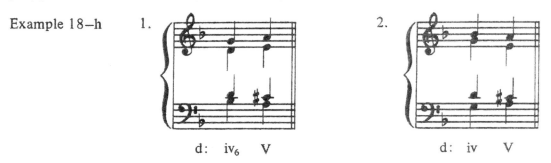

Baroque composers frequently used the phrygian cadence to conclude a movement of an extended work and to provide a transition into the next movement. Example 18–i illustrates the use of a phrygian cadence in F minor, concluding a movement. The subsequent movement is in F major.

The phrygian cadence derives its name from the Phrygian mode.

Example 18–i

"And With His Stripes" from *Messiah*

Handel

The *deceptive cadence*[1] is a cadence in which a chord (usually the submediant) has been used in place of the tonic triad. The progression involved in this cadence is generally V–vi.

Example 18–j

1.

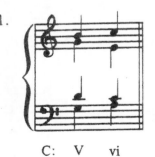

C: V vi

2.

c: V VI

The use of the deceptive cadence creates cadential variety, as in example 18–k.

_____

[1] The deceptive cadence is sometimes referred to as the evaded cadence.

Example 18–k

Chorale: *"Christ lag in Todesbanden"*   J. S. Bach

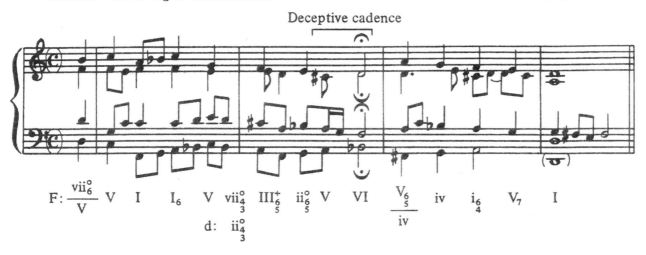

Composers have also used the deceptive cadence to extend the concluding measures of a work.

Example 18–l

Invention in D Major, concluding measures   Bach

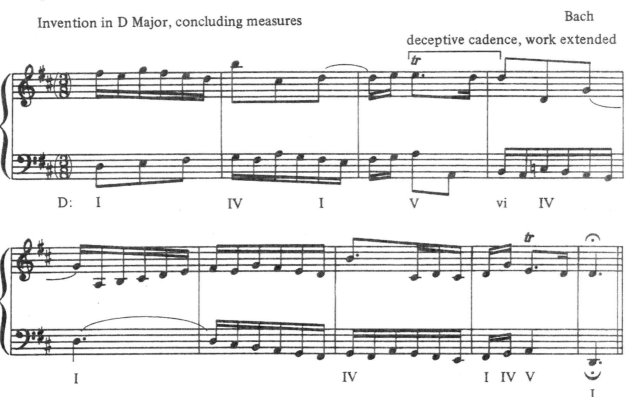

As in example 18–l, composers have most often caused the final chord of the concluding cadence to fall on an accented beat, creating a *rhythmic cadence* as well as a harmonic cadence. The terms "masculine cadence" and "feminine cadence" are sometimes applied to cadences which fall on strong beats and weak beats, respectively.

Keyboard Assignment 18

Play in four voices, the following cadences in all major and minor keys through four sharps and four flats.

a. Perfect Authentic Cadence.
b. Imperfect Authentic Cadence.
c. Perfect Plagal Cadence.
d. Imperfect Plagal Cadence.
e. Half Cadence.
f. Phrygian Cadence (minor keys only).
g. Deceptive Cadence.

CHAPTER 19

Principles of Harmonic Progression

Each musical style period develops a distinct "sound ideal." The characteristic sound of a style is the result of the exchange of ideas among composers, the social function of music in a particular culture, and the development of musical instruments.

The sound ideal of the eighteenth century included, among many other elements, a characteristic manner in which harmonic progressions were used. Each triad and seventh chord in eighteenth century music has a fairly well defined function which it fulfills. Therefore, twentieth century theorists speak of eighteenth century harmony as *"functional harmony."* In the analysis of harmonic progressions, the *root movements* found in a work are of primary concern to the theorist. A root movement is the interval between the root of a chord and the root of the subsequent chord to which it progresses in a musical phrase. Root movement is different from interval in the bass line, and the two coincide only when chords are in root position.

The *basic root movements* found in eighteenth century music and which are therefore considered to be *progressions* in those styles are as follows:

1. Any triad or diatonic seventh (and many altered chords) may be found moving down a fifth,[1] up a second, or down a third.[2]

2. The tonic triad may be found moving to any triad in the key, regardless of root movement.

3. Any triad may be found moving to the *tonic* or to the *dominant* triads.

4. The leading-tone triad (vii°) is seldom found moving to any triad other than the tonic. Exception to this generally involves a series of root movements resolving down in fifths (I–IV–vii°–iii–vi–ii–V–I).

Exceptions to these basic root movements are occasionally found. These exceptions, called *retrogressions*, generally involve a high degree of melodic interest in the individual voices or a series of chords in first inversion, with the bass moving scalewise, as illustrated in example 17–i. Another exception, found occasionally, is the root movement V–IV followed by V or I.

---

[1] This root movement is rather arbitrarily designated "down a fifth" instead of up a fourth.

[2] These root movements, which may be considered to be basic, are those which will both prepare (by sounding in the same voice in the preceding chord) and provide for the scalewise resolution, down, of the seventh of a seventh chord, as discussed in Chapter 23. It is perhaps significant that composers' preference for the three basic root movements and their use of seventh chords developed concurrently, during the Baroque period. Furthermore, it may be that these root movements were used for triads because these root movements provide a resolution for the seventh harmonic.

Example 19—a

Chorale: *"Werde Munter, mein Gemüte"*

Bach

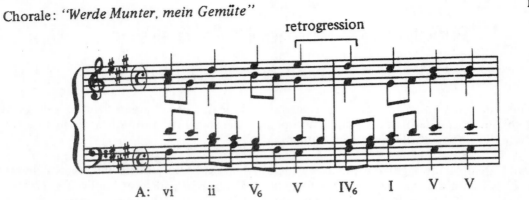

A root movement from vi to V is covered by point 3, above (movement to the dominant), but this particular down a second root movement is so often used that it deserves special emphasis. The following example illustrates this root movement, which can be found throughout the common practice period, but is especially prominent in the music of Beethoven.

Example 19—b

Sonata in E Minor, Op. 90

Beethoven

The retrogression ii moving to vi is sometimes found in music literature, and is usually the result of the repetition of a melodic pattern at a different pitch level (a sequence, see chapter 24).

Example 19–c

Sonata in C Major, Op. 53   Beethoven

C: I   V   ii   vi   IV   I   V   I

Harmonic rhythm is a term which refers to the *rate* of *change* of *harmony* and is an important element in a composer's style. Harmonic rhythm may be fast or slow, regular or irregular, with a different musical effect resulting from the combination of these variables. The Bach chorales, being rather slow and majestic in quality, have a fast, regular harmonic rhythm. The Concerto Grosso by Handel, found in Chapter 12, has a slow, fairly regular harmonic rhythm in the movements marked Allegro. An irregular harmonic rhythm can result in a restless, dramatic effect, such as is often found in nineteenth century works.

Eighteenth century composers typically maintained or even increased the harmonic rhythm at cadences. The *Allemande* from which example 19–d is quoted maintains a harmonic rhythm of one or two chords in each measure. In the final measure, the harmonic rhythm is increased to four chords on two beats.

Example 19–d

Allemande, from *French Suite in E Major*   Bach

harmonic rhythm increased

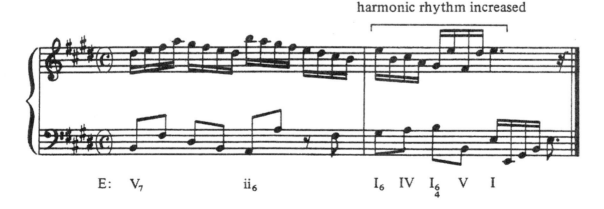

E: V_7 ii_6 I_6 IV I_6^4 V I

Likewise, Bach maintained or increased the harmonic rhythm at cadences in harmonizing chorales. Choral phrases often close with a half-note, or with a repeated quarter-note on the supertonic moving to the tonic. Bach generally maintains the harmonic rhythm at this point by using a 4–3 suspension (example 19–e) or by using a supertonic to dominant progression (example 19–f).

Example 19–e

Chorale: *"Weg, mein Herz, mit dem Gedanken"*   Bach

G: I   V₆   IV₆   I   V₄₂   I₆   V   I

The harmonic rhythm is often maintained by use of a supertonic to dominant harmony.

Example 19–f

Chorale: *"Du Friedefürst, Herr Jesu Christ"*   Bach

A: vi   V   I   V₆   IV₆   I₆₄   ii₆₅   V   I

Harmonizing the supertonic in the melody with two counts of dominant sonority in the absence of a suspension is not characteristic of the style.

Example 19–g

A: IV₆   I   V   I

Although the augmented fourth, when used melodically in a progression, is generally outside the eighteenth century style, the inversion of this interval, the diminished fifth, occurs with some frequency, especially in the progression IV–V₆.

114

Example 19–h

Chorale: *"Gelobet seist du, Jesu Christ"*   Bach

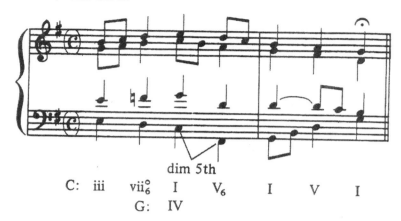

dim 5th

C: iii   vii°₆   I   V₆   I   V   I
G: IV

Steps in the harmonization of a chorale melody:

1. Sing or play each phrase several times in order to determine the key best suited for its harmonization. This may or may not be the key of the signature.

2. Determine which of the cadence types will successfully complete each phrase. (If there is no cadence possible in the key selected, another choice of key should be made.)

3. Select triads which will result in effective root movements. Each note which is to be harmonized in this chapter's problems may be either the root, third, or fifth of a triad. At the same time, the melodic quality of the bass line is to be given equal consideration. Create a bass line that moves scalewise as much as possible, through careful use of inversions. Maintain harmonic rhythm throughout each phrase.

4. Add the inner voices.

5. Play the work on the piano.

Topic for Class Discussion

Discuss the root movement logic or lack of logic in the progressions and retrogressions shown below. The symbols are shown for major tonality, but the root movements for minor tonality are the same, except for the III+ chord, which is almost non-existent. III in minor would appear on this chart only in its major form (see Chapter 17).

Frequent root movement	*possible root movement*	*unlikely root movement*
I moving to ii, iii, IV, V, vi, vii°₆		
ii moving to V, iii, vii°₆, I	ii moving to vi	ii moving to IV
iii moving to vi, IV, I	iii moving to V	iii moving to vii°₆, ii
IV moving to vii°₆, V, ii, I		IV moving to iii, vi
V moving to I, vi, iii	V moving to IV, ii	V moving to vii°₆ (harmless, but not strong)
vi moving to ii, vii°₆, IV, V	vi moving to I	vi moving to iii
vii°₆ moving to I	vii°₆ moving to iii, vi (vi substituting for I)	vii°₆ moving to ii, IV, V (vii°₆ to V is harmless, but not strong)

Instructional note: Memorizing the chart is not as important as *understanding* the chart.

Question Frequently Asked

Question: Why did the composers not double the fifth in writing root position triads?

Answer: There are two reasons for this. When the fifth is doubled, the "hollow" fifth interval is reinforced and emphasized. Also, in moving out of a chord that has a doubled fifth, the composer has a greatly increased chance to write undesirable parallels than would be the case if the fifth is not doubled. There would have to be compelling horizontal (melodic) reasons that would cause an eighteenth century composer to double the fifth in a root position triad.

Keyboard Assignment 19

a.   Play the following progressions in all major and minor keys, around the circle of fifths.

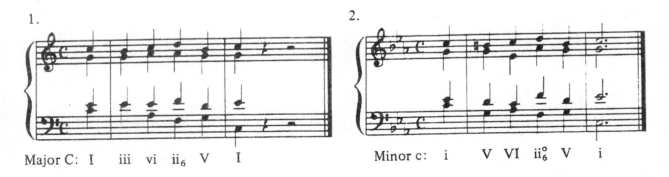

Major C: I   iii   vi   ii₆   V   I   Minor c: i   V   VI   ii°₆   V   i

116

b. Play the following progression in G, D, A, E, F, Bb, and Eb major.

C: I   V   I   IV₆   I₆   IV   vii°₆   I

c. Play the following progression in C, A, E, and D minor.

c: i   V₆   i   iv₆   i₆   IV   vii°₆   i

CHAPTER 20

Diatonic Common Chord Modulation

Modulation is a process which results in a change in key center. The most frequently encountered form of modulation in Baroque literature is the *diatonic common chord modulation*.[1] In this type of modulation, a composer uses a diatonic chord called a *"pivot"* chord which functions in both the original key and the key to which the modulation leads. This chord is spelled the same in both keys. The analysis of a diatonic common chord modulation is illustrated in example 20—a.

Example 20—a

Chorale: *"Ach, bleib bei uns, Herr Jesu Christ"*

Bach

The pivot chord in a diatonic common chord modulation is generally the chord immediately preceding the first accidental.

Related keys differ by one sharp or flat in their key signature, including both major and minor keys. Thus there are five keys related to any given key. The keys related to a major key are represented by the diatonic major and minor triads found within that key. The keys related to a minor key are represented by the diatonic major and minor triads found within that minor key's relative major.

Contiguous keys in the circle of fifths are related. In example 20—b, the keys related to either A minor or C major are enclosed.

Example 20—b

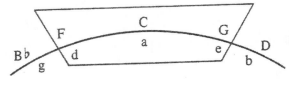

---

[1] Two other types of modulation in tonal music are the chromatic modulation and the enharmonic modulation. These are discussed in *Harmony, Baroque to Contemporary, Part II*.

It is doubtful that a *modulation* can be made to occur without the use of accidentals foreign to the original key. The "modulation" in example 20-c probably does not occur, because the ear heard no tone foreign to the key of C.

Example 20-c

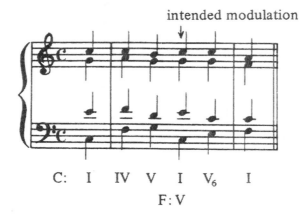

In order to establish a new key, composers usually use a sub-dominant type chord (ii or IV) and a dominant type chord (V or vii°) in the new key. Example 20-d does establish F as a new tonal center.

Example 20-d

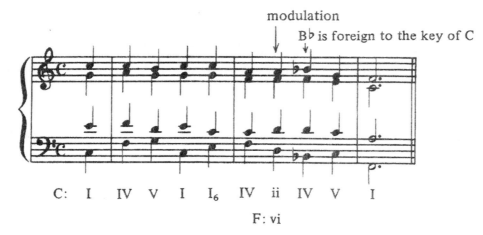

Typically, though perhaps not in every case, a modulation will involve a cadence in the key to which the modulation moves.

A modulation in which the tonal center remains, but the mode changes from major to minor or from minor to major is called a *"change of mode."* The relationship between the two keys is designated *"parallel major"* or *"parallel minor."* This type of modulation was used occasionally by Baroque composers and was used with increasing frequency by composers writing in the late eighteenth century and in the nineteenth century.

The relationship between the two minuets from the Suite in E♭ Major by Bach illustrates the use of a change of mode to the parallel minor. The first minuet closes in E♭ major.

Example 20—e

Suite in E♭ Major

Bach

The second minuet is written in E♭ minor.

Example 20—f

Suite in E♭ Major

Bach

A phrase may begin in a new key without the use of a pivot chord. This *"phrase modulation"* is somewhat rare.

Example 20—g

Chorale: *"Kyrie, Gott Vater in Ewigkeit"*

Bach

phrase modulation

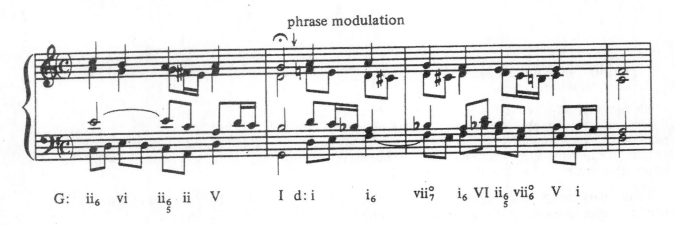

G: ii₆ vi ii₆₅ ii V   I d:i   i₆   vii°₇ i₆ VI ii₆₅ vii°₆ V i

Questions Frequently Asked

Question: Is it legal for an octave to be retained in connecting two triads?

Answer: First of all, we must deal with the concept of "legality." Do not think in terms of laws and rules. There are probably no rules that apply to all musical styles. The composers of the Common Practice Period wrote what they and their patrons wanted to hear, pursuing a "sound ideal," without reference to a rule-book. They were consistent about many things, and this has given rise to the rule concept of teaching and learning music theory. It is far better to understand *why* the composers did what they did, because this allows the student to develop rational and aesthetic judgment that can be applied to many style periods. Dealing with the heart of your question, the answer is "yes." The octave relationship does no harm to the independence of the voices until the two voices *move* together in an octave.

Question: May the voices overlap; that is, may the bass move to a note higher than the tenor voice was in the preceding chord, or the soprano voice move to a note lower than the alto voice was in the preceding chord?

Answer: Most of these overlap problems can be solved by arranging the voices so that they may move to the nearest chord tone (the horizontal element) that gives strong doubling (the vertical element). The following example may clarify this:

Example 20–h

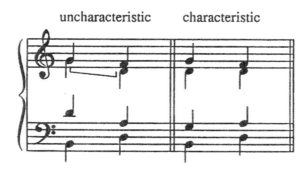

However, Bach, the greatest of the partwriters, frequently allows the bass to overlap the tenor when the root movement is down a fifth.

Example 20–i

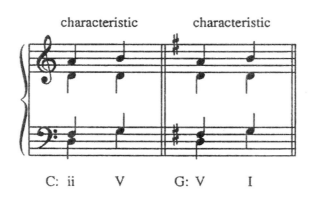

121

Question: From time to time, we hear comments about "hidden fifths" and "hidden octaves"; that is, moving into a fifth or octave, both voices moving in the same direction. Are these examples outside the style?

Example 20–j

Answer: The confusion on this point arises from bringing concepts that pertain to eighteenth century two-voice counterpoint into four-voice writing. Two-voice counterpoint is "fragile," and therefore more conservative than three- or four-voice writing. In example—a, above, if only the upper two voices exist, the eighteenth century composers thought of that approach to a perfect fifth as an undesirable sound. When a third or fourth voice was added, the approach to a fifth in similar motion is not noticed by the listener. Similarly, in example—b above, if only the tenor and bass exist, the composers avoided that effect. But when the upper two voices are added, the sound is within the style.

Question: Can all voices move in the same direction in a progression, as in example–c above?

Answer: Yes. If it *is* a problem, it is self-correcting, because it is almost impossible for the next progression to continue with all voices moving down. Keep in mind that if the composers of the Common Practice Period would have followed all the rules taught by many theorists, the composers could have written only a small portion of their actual production.

Question: Why is changing structure an error?

Answer: Maintaining structure, either open or close, has no virtue in itself. In four-part, root position writing, a change of structure can cause partwriting errors.

Question: Do all the triads appear in approximately the same frequency?

Answer: No, the triads used most frequently are I, IV, and V, the primary triads. Used almost as frequently are ii and vii$^o_6$. The iii and vi are used less often. The frequently used triads are strongly tonal and are not highly colorful. The iii and vi triads are not strongly tonal, but are highly colorful.

Question: Why did the Common Practice Period composers restrict their uses of second inversions?

Answer: The composers, and their patrons, heard the interval of a fourth above the bass as a dissonance, demanding resolution to the interval of a third above the bass, which is achieved in the cadential and pedal $\frac{6}{4}$ patterns.

Question: Why did the composers restrict their use of iii$_6$ and vi$_6$?

Answer: The effect of vi$_6$ is that of I with an added sixth, and the effect of iii$_6$ is that of V with an added sixth.

Example 20–k

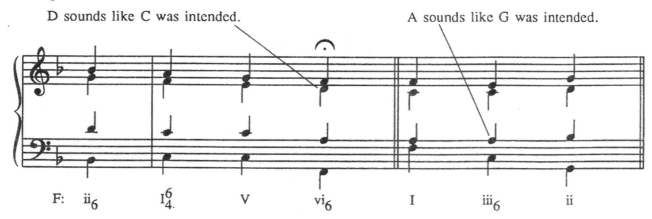

D sounds like C was intended.   A sounds like G was intended.

F: ii$_6$ I$^6_4$ V   vi$_6$ I   iii$_6$ ii

Triads with added sixths were not part of the eighteenth century style, although there was at that time much discussion about the first inversion seventh chord as a triad with added sixth.

C: ii$^6_5$

Keyboard Assignment 20

a. Play five separate modulations from G major to each of its related keys, in eighteenth century four-part style (without the use of written aids). Analyze as you play. The following steps are recommended.

1. Before beginning to play, mentally select the pivot chord.

2. Establish the key of G, using I IV V I or a similar progression.

3. Move to the pivot chord.

4. Establish the new key.

b. Modulate from D minor to each of its related keys. Establish, by using suitable harmonic progressions, D minor, and each related key.

CHAPTER 21

The Classic Period and Sonata Allegro Form

The Baroque period reached a climax in the second decade of the eighteenth century with the works of Bach and Handel. From that point in time, and continuing for some fifty years, there occurred a transitional period called the *"Rococo"* in architecture and painting, and the *"gallant"* style in music. The gallant style represents a reaction against what the new generation of composers regarded as unnecessary polyphonic complexity in the music of their predecessors. The gallant style embodied an impulse toward simplicity and "prettiness." Some of the characteristics of this style were continued into the Classic period (1750-1800); most notably, the pianistic figuration known as *"Alberti bass,"* named for the composer Domenico Alberti (1717?-1740). This accompaniment

figure ♪ and other similar patterns are common in the keyboard works of the

principal Classic composers, Haydn (1732-1809) and Mozart (1756-1791), and in the early works of Beethoven (1770-1827). The Alberti bass and its equivalent orchestral patterns served the function of animating a harmony rhythmically, while avoiding the addition of contrapuntal figures which might make a work more difficult to play and to comprehend.

The forms of particular importance in the Classic period were the symphony, the solo concerto, the overture, the string quartet and chamber music in general, the solo sonata (whose form differed from that of the Baroque sonata), opera, art song, and the concert mass.

During the transition from the Baroque to the Classic, several instruments fell into disuse: the recorder was superseded by the flute; the viols by the violin family (except for the bass viol); and the clavichord, harpsichord, and lute by the piano.

The pipe organ entered a period of decline in the Classic period relative to the quality of the instruments built, the technique of performers, and the amount of music composed. There were few significant works written in the Classic period for the organ, in contrast to the large number of organ works written in the Baroque period.

The playing of brass instruments also declined. The horn and trumpet parts in a classic symphony typically were limited to the occasional "punctuation" of the tonic and dominant harmony.

Reflecting the aristocratic society for which they worked, the classic composers created works notable for their elegance, restraint, and occasional subtle humor.

Classic composers used the principles of harmonic progression found in the Baroque period, the difference between the Baroque and Classic periods being more a difference in application of basic principles than in harmonic vocabulary. For example, the sixth and fourth above the bass in the cadential $\frac{6}{4}$ pattern in Classic compositions often move up to the fifth and seventh of the dominant seventh.[1]

---

[1] Other characteristics of the Classic period are discussed in Chapter 24.

Example 21—a

Sonata in F Major, K. 332   Mozart

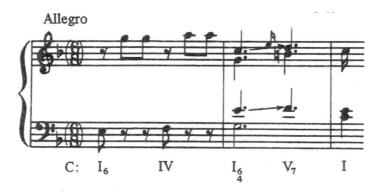

Classic composers occasionally wrote parallel octaves by contrary motion between the outer voices in authentic cadences, especially in their keyboard works. This is in contrast to Baroque literature, where this effect is not found.

Example 21—b

Sonata No. 5 in C minor, Op. 10, No. 1   Beethoven
(concluding measures, First Movement)

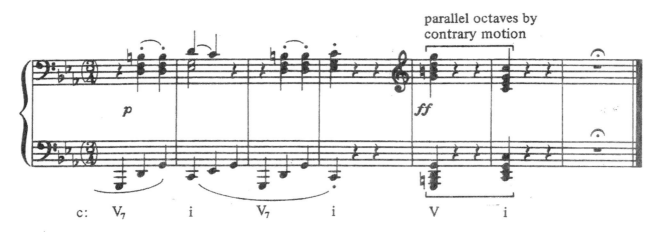

Significant musical developments during the Classic period include the evolution of the symphony orchestra with fairly standard, basic instrumentation and the evolution of the Classic sonata form. The sonata form is a three movement (in solo sonatas and concertos) or four movement (in symphonies and most chamber works) plan which provides for considerable contrast in tempo and mood between the movements. Generally, the first movement, and often the last movement, of a symphony, concerto, or sonata is written in a form called *"Sonata Allegro."* This form may be outlined as follows:

Example 21—c

Exposition	Introduction: Optional, frequently slow in tempo. First Subject: Usually vigorous, in the tonic key. Bridge or transition: Modulates, usually to the key of the dominant if the work is in a major key or to the related major if the work is in minor. Second Subject: Often more lyric than was the first subject. The key is that prepared by the bridge, or transition. Closing Theme and/or Coda: May be new material, but often is derived from the first subject. The key is generally that of the second subject. The exposition typically is enclosed in double bar–repeat symbols.
Development	This section presents the material from the exposition in ways not used before in the work. The development typically modulates freely. Occasionally, new material is found in development sections.
Recapitulation	The material originally heard in the exposition reappears, entirely in the tonic key. The development and recapitulation sections are generally enclosed together by double bar–repeat signs.

The following "sonata allegro" forms are included for class discussion and analysis.

Example 21–d

Piano Sonata in F Major, First Movement   Haydn

[Allegro moderato]

Example 21-e

Divertimento I, K. 439 B, First Movement

Mozart

---

[2] Clarinets sound a M2 lower than written.

[3] A bassoon part in the key of C has been included so that the example may be played on the piano.

134

(There is no specific keyboard assignment for this chapter.)

Questions Frequently Asked

Question: Were the Classic composers aware of the sonata allegro form; that is, did they consciously create this form, or did the form "just happen" as they wrote?

Answer: There is some controversy about this, but my opinion is, they were totally aware of what they were doing. These were people having an extremely high musical intelligence, awareness, and sensitivity. They were working during the period of European history known as the "Enlightenment," when intellectuals were trying to understand *everything.* If one of Mozart's students asked him to explain why so many of the first movements of his sonatas and symphonies have a similar design, or form, it cannot be believed that Mozart would have had to admit that he did not know what he was doing. Prolific composers of every style period have relied upon forms and procedures that have been successful for the composer in prior compositions. The sonata allegro form is but one of these—there are others: rounded binary, ternary and various rondo forms.

Question: I have read that the first textbook references to the sonata allegro form appeared in the 1830s.[1] Doesn't that indicate that the Classic composers were writing this form intuitively?

Answer: No, it indicates that authors of theory books are usually a generation or two behind the composers who define a style. Also, it is difficult to prove that something *doesn't* exist; in this case, perhaps the form was described prior to 1830, and the reference was lost. In fact, a paragraph[2] written by Johann Adolph Scheibe (1708-1776) describes the sonata allegro form exactly as we do today, except the modulation is said to be to "the key of the fifth," if major, and "the key of the third," if minor, instead of "dominant" and "related major." A further proof that the composers consciously controlled the sonata allegro form is found in the tonal design of the movement. The modulation to the dominant or related major for the second subject would be expected to appear in only 20% of the sonatas if "chance" were the controlling factor, and the other related keys would each appear in 20% of the sonatas, there being five keys related to the original. That the other related keys (not to mention unrelated keys) do not appear in the statement of the second subject in the exposition is further proof that the composers were conscious of the thematic and tonal design they were creating.

Question: Did all the classic composers use the sonata allegro form in the same way?

Answer: No, and it should not be expected that they would, for the sonata form is not a straight-jacket, but rather, it is a basic design. Haydn, for example, in perhaps three out of four of his piano sonatas, uses motives (short melodic ideas) in the second theme that are derived from the first theme. Mozart also does this, but less frequently. Another difference is found in the writing of the recapitulation in sonatas in minor keys. The second theme in the exposition of a sonata in, for example, C minor, would be expected to be in E flat major. In the recapitulation of a Mozart or Haydn sonata, this second theme will appear in C minor, but Beethoven does not typically "minorize" this second subject; instead the second theme will usually appear in C major, the tonic key, but major mode. In another instance, the Sonata in D Major, K. 311, which appears in the Book II workbook, Mozart reversed the order of the subjects in the recapitulation.

---

[1] See, for example, Donald Jay Grout, *A History of Western Music,* 3rd ed. New York: W. W. Norton, 1980, p. 460.

[2] The entire passage, and several other 18th century descriptions of the sonata allegro form, are quoted in the dissertation: Nancy Kovaleff Baker, "From *Teil* to *Tonstück:* The Significance of the *Versuch einer anleitung zur Composition* by Heirich Christoph Koch," (Ph.D. dissertation, Yale University, 1975).

CHAPTER 22

Non-Harmonic Tones

Non-harmonic tones are those tones in a musical texture which are not chord members. Non-harmonic tones are classified by their manner of approach and their manner of resolution.

The *passing tone* is a non-harmonic tone which is approached scalewise and resolved scalewise, continuing in the same direction.

Example 22—a

The passing tone may be unaccented (occurring off the beat) as in example 22—a or accented (occurring on the beat) as show in example 22—b.

Passing tones may be single, as in examples 22—a and 22—b or double or triple, as in example 22—c.

Example 22—c

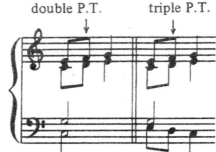

Baroque and Classic composers often combined non-harmonic tones so that two or three occurred simultaneously. These non-harmonic tones characteristically combine in a consonant interval or in a triadic relationship.

Generally, eighteenth century composers did not use a passing tone interpolated between two perfect fifths.

Example 22—d

The Baroque and Classic composers seldom allowed a perfect fifth formed by a passing tone to move into another perfect fifth.

Example 22—e

The problem arising in example 22—e was characteristically solved by the use of irregular doubling.

Example 22—f

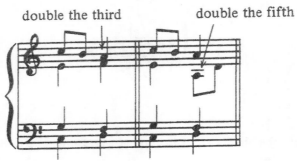

A passing tone may be chromatic, moving by half-step.

Example 22—g

Altered passing tones are often found in Baroque and Classic style.

Example 22–h

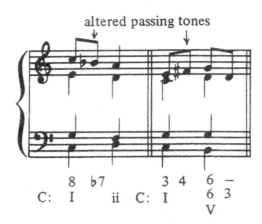

The 3–2 passing tone over the dominant was *seldom* used by Baroque composers in four-voice writing.

Example 22–i

The *suspension* is a non-harmonic tone that is approached by preparation and resolved scalewise, usually down. Suspensions almost always occur on a stronger beat, or portion of beat, than does the resolution. Except in the 9–8 suspension, the note of resolution of a suspension is seldom sounded in another voice simultaneous with the suspension.[1]

The *9–8 suspension* is generally found where the root movement is up a second and generally involves a triad in root position.

Example 22–j

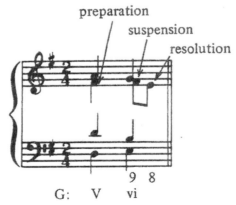

---

[1] While this is almost always true in choral music, it is less the case in instrumental music. In the more dissonant of Bach's organ music, the note of resolution does occasionally occur with the suspension. See the Prelude in E Minor —the "Cathedral."

However, it is possible for the chord to change as the suspension resolves.

Example 22–k

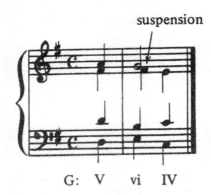

In a keyboard or instrumental style, the suspension illustrated in example 22–k above might appear as in example 22–l.

Example 22–l

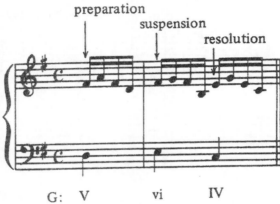

In the 9–8 suspension, the note of resolution is present at the time that the suspension occurs.

The *7–6 suspension* often occurs over the leading tone triad.

Example 22–m

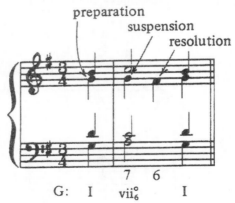

The 7–6 suspension occurs over a first inversion triad and the note of resolution is not characteristically present in another voice as the suspension occurs.

The *4–3 suspension* often involves the progression I–V.

140

Example 22—n

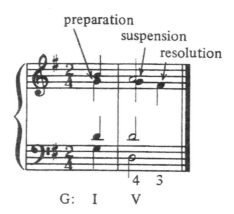

The 4—3 suspension occurs over a root position triad, and the note of resolution is not characteristically present in another voice as the suspension occurs.

The *2—1 suspension* may occasionally be found. It is usually an open structure version of the 9—8 suspension.

Example 22—o

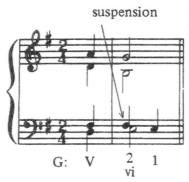

The *2-3 suspension* results when the bass note is suspended. The note of resolution is typically the chord third, not the root or fifth. Two different figured bass systems are used to indicate this suspension, as shown in example 22-p.

Example 22—p

Chorale: *"Aus meines Herzens Grunde"*   Bach

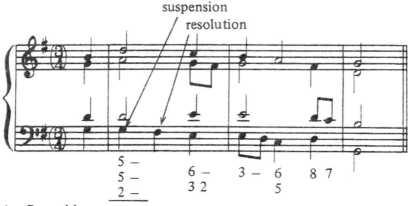

Suspensions almost invariably resolve downward in the chorale style and in choral music in general. In keyboard and instrumental writing, occasional use is made of **upward resolving** suspensions, *retardations.* This upward resolving suspension usually occurs at cadences.

Example 22–q

Sonata in B♭, K. 281, First Movement

Mozart

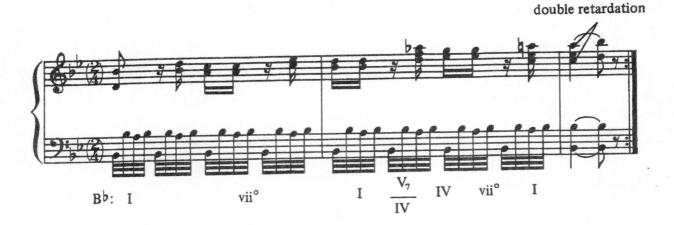

double retardation

B♭: I   vii°   I $\dfrac{V_7}{IV}$ IV   vii°   I

One further suspension is a special case, a 5–4 suspension over the tonic $\frac{6}{4}$ chord. This suspension is used infrequently, and is typically found in cadence patterns.

Example 22–r

Chorale: *"Jesus Christus, unser Heiland, der von uns"*

Bach

G: I   vii°₆   i₆⁄₄   V   i

e: ii°₆

Although suspensions may occur in any voice, most occur in the alto.

The suspension may be ornamented in its resolution.

142

Example 22—s

Chorale: *"Ein Lämmlein geht und trägt die Schuld"*   Bach

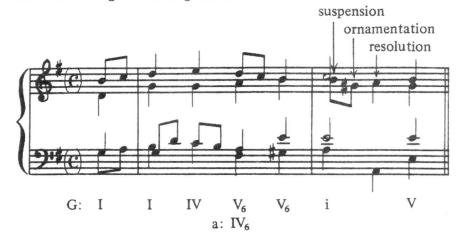

G: I   I   IV   V₆   V₆   i   V

a: IV₆

A suspended note may be tied from the note of preparation or it may be repeated. In choral music, the choice is made on the basis of need for a note for a syllable of text. In organ music, however, suspensions are almost always tied, there being no need to restrike tones in order to prolong them. When the note of preparation is of shorter duration than the suspension, the tones are seldom tied in Baroque technique, as in example 22—t—1. The augmented second is never found used in the ornamental resolution of a suspension in minor keys, as in example 22—t—2.

Example 22—t

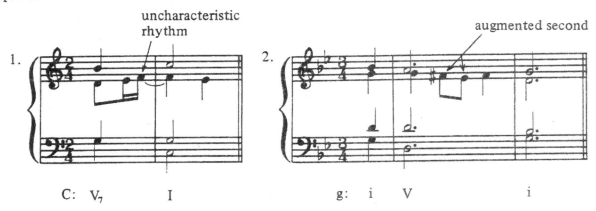

C: V₇   I   g: i   V   i

The *neighboring tone* is a non-harmonic tone which is approached scalewise and resolved scalewise in a direction opposite to the approach. The neighboring tone may be upper or lower; single, double, or triple; diatonic or altered. It is frequently used, in four-voice writing, where the chord is repeated and no other non-harmonic tones can be used conveniently.

143

Example 22—u

Chorale: *"Erbarm dich mein, o Herre Gott"*   Bach

neighboring tone

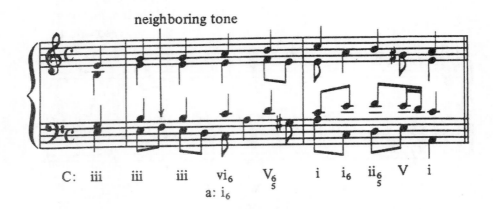

C: iii   iii   iii   vi₆   V₆₅   i   i₆   ii₆₅   V   i

a: i₆

There is a tendency to alter neighboring tones, particularly lower neighboring tones, so that they involve a minor second. This sometimes produces a simultaneous cross-relation between the neighboring tone and a chord member, as shown in example 22—v.

Example 22—v

Concerto in D Minor, K. 466   Mozart

simultaneous cross relation

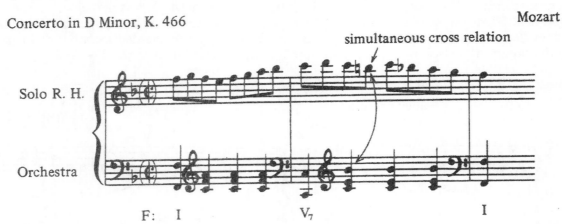

Solo R. H.

Orchestra

F: I   V₇   I

The *appoggiatura*[2] is a non-harmonic tone that is approached by a leap and resolved scalewise, usually in the direction opposite to the approach. The appoggiatura may fall on the beat or on an unaccented portion of the beat, and may, on occasion, be found resolving in the direction of the approach.

---

[2] This use of the term "appoggiatura" differs from its use as the Baroque and Classic ornament, which was a dissonance occuring on a beat, and was written as a small (grace) note so that the harmony might be more readily perceived. The "appoggiatura" in the following example is an accented passing tone.

Sonata in C Major, K. 309, Third Movement   Mozart

"appoggiatura"   accented passing tone

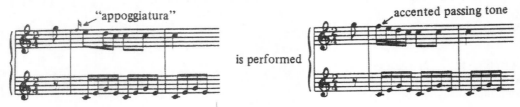

is performed

144

Example 22—w

Chorale: *"Aus tiefer Not schrei ich zu dir"*   Bach

appoggiatura

G: ii   vi   IV   I   IV   I$_6^4$ V$_7$ I

The appoggiatura is far more frequently found in keyboard and instrumental music than in choral music because of the degree of risk involved in requiring singers to approach a dissonance by a leap. The appoggiatura is occasionally approached by an augmented fourth, as in example 22—x.

Example 22—x

Sonata in C Major   Haydn

appoggiaturas are marked with arrows

augmented fourth

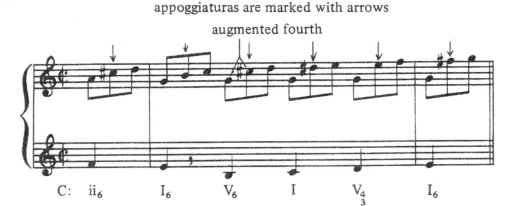

C: ii$_6$ I$_6$ V$_6$ I   V$_4^3$ I$_6$

The *escape tone* (also called *échappée*) is a non-harmonic tone which is approached scalewise and resolved by a leap in the direction opposite to the approach. The leap involved in the escape tone pattern is generally a third. In chorales, the escape tone is typically used in the soprano voice, at the cadence. The escape tone generally falls on an unaccented portion of a beat.

Example 22—y

Chorale: *"Ach Gott und Herr"*   Bach

escape tone

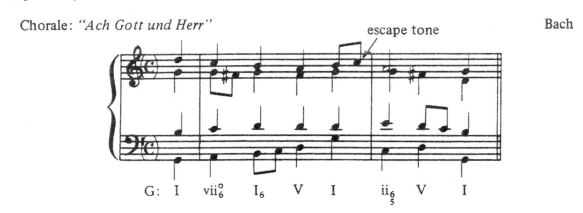

G: I   vii°$_6$ I$_6$ V   I   ii$_6^5$ V   I

145

Example 22–z illustrates a use of the escape tone which is not in eighteenth century style.

Example 22–z

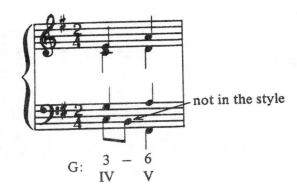

The *pedal tone* is a non-harmonic tone which is approached by preparation and is resolved by being retained. This non-harmonic tone is practically non-existent in chorales, but is of frequent occurrence is eighteenth century keyboard and instrumental music. Chords sounding above a pedal tone are found used in any inversion.

Example 22–aa

Example 16–o, measure two, illustrates the use of a pedal tone in keyboard music.

The *anticipation* is a non-harmonic tone which is generally approached scalewise and is resolved by being retained. In chorales, the anticipation is typically used at the cadence in the soprano part. Double anticipations are possible, as another part moves with the soprano in parallel thirds or sixths.

Example 22–bb

Chorale: *"Werde munter, mein Gemüte"*   Bach

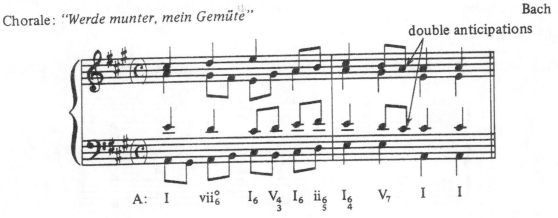

Parallel fifths formed by the combination of an anticipation and an 8–7 passing tone are found in the Bach chorales and are considered to be within the eighteenth century style.

Example 22—cc

Chorale: *"Freuet euch, ihr Christen alle"*   Bach

In the eighteenth century, anticipations were seldom used throughout the phrase in the lower three voices.

Although the typical anticipation is retained and resolved as a chord tone, occasionally an anticipation occurs and is retained as a non-harmonic tone; which, by definition becomes a suspension, since it is prepared.

Example 22—dd

Piano Sonata, Op. 7   Beethoven

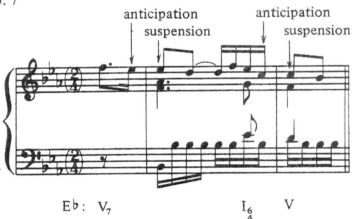

The designation *"changing tones"* may be given to any two non-harmonic tones a third apart which resolve to the intervening note, which will characteristically be a chord tone. This use of the term changing tone would include the passing tone with ornamentation, the neighboring tone with ornamentation, and the appoggiatura with ornamentation.

147

Example 22—ee

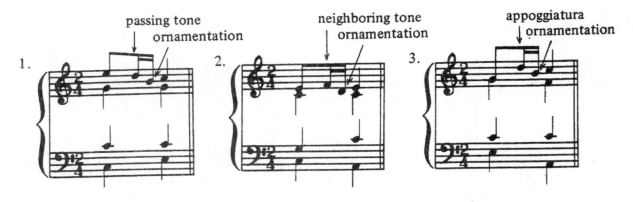

The *nota cambiata* is a non-harmonic tone designation which had various meanings during the past two centuries. To some musicologists and theorists *nota cambiata* describes all of the changing tone patterns in example 22—ee, while to others, it is applicable only to the soprano pattern in example 22—ee—1.

A non-harmonic tone approached by leap and departed by leap is a *free tone*, and if no clear resolution exists for this dissonance, it is outside eighteenth century technique.

Example 22—ff

free tone, not in the style

Keyboard Assignment 22

a. Play the following progressions in all major keys through four sharps and four flats.

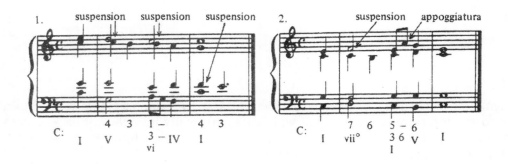

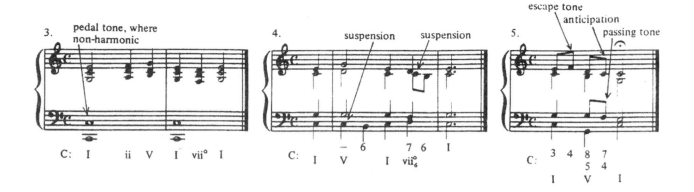

b. Play the progressions in a.; 2., 4., and 5., in all (harmonic) minor keys through three sharps and flats.

c. Play the progression in a. 1., above in all minor keys. Employ the descending form of the melodic minor scale in the alto voice.

CHAPTER 23

The Dominant Seventh

The dominant triad becomes the *dominant seventh chord* with the addition of a tone a minor third above the triad's fifth.

Example 23—a

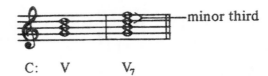

This seventh chord is designated "major-minor seventh chord" (abbreviated Mm7). The triad is major and the distance from the root to the seventh is a minor seventh when the triad is arranged in root position.

The seventh of the dominant seventh chord was considered a dissonance by eighteenth century composers. For this reason, they generally approached and resolved the seventh with care.

The approach to the seventh of the V_7 is most often by *preparation*, that is, by retaining that tone in the same voice from the immediately preceding chord. The basic root movements (down a fifth, up a second, and down a third) will prepare the seventh of any seventh chord and will allow the seventh to resolve down scalewise to a chord tone, which is the most characteristic resolution.

Example 23—b

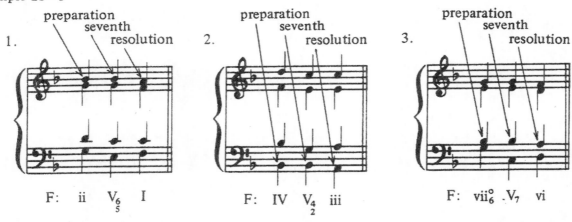

| Approach: Roots a fifth apart | Roots a second apart | Roots a third apart |
| Resolution: Roots a fifth apart | Roots a third apart | Roots a second apart |

Approaching the V_7 from vii° (example 23—b—3) is not particularly characteristic; because of the strong similarity in the sound of the two chords, there is almost no forward movement in the harmony in the progression vii°–V, or vii°–V_7.

Example 23—b illustrates that the dominant seventh chord may be approached and resolved by employing the basic root movements. The seventh of a seventh chord exerts a strong downward pull, as it is used in the eighteenth century style. The approach and resolution of the seventh in the manner illustrated in example 23–b treats the seventh like a suspension.

In addition to the approaches to the seventh of the V_7 illustrated in example 23–b, the seventh may be approached like a passing tone, as in example 23–c.

Example 23–c

Chorale: *"Gott lebet noch"*   Bach

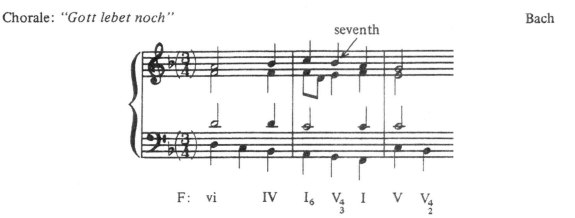

The seventh of the V_7 may be approached like a neighboring tone, scalewise from below.

Example 23–d

Chorale: *"Jesu meine Freude"*   Bach

The seventh of the V_7 may be approached like an appoggiatura, by leap.

Example 23–e

Brandenburg Concerto, No. I, Minuet   Bach

151

In eighteenth century styles, the appoggiatura approach to the seventh is generally from below the seventh and is usually the interval of a third.

In a *regular resolution* the seventh resolves downward immediately to the tone of resolution in the same voice, as in examples 23—a through 23—e. However, there are some *irregular resolutions* of the dominant seventh in eighteenth century styles.

In an *ornamental resolution* the seventh of a seventh chord may move to one or more tones before resolving. Typically, in this resolution, the seventh chord is retained until the resolution of the seventh has occurred.

Example 23—f

Rondo, K. 494   Mozart

In a *delayed resolution* the seventh of a seventh chord is retained as a non-dissonant chord member in a new harmony, it then becomes the seventh of the V_7, then it finally resolves.

Example 23—g

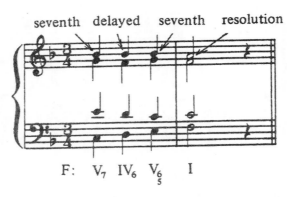

In a *transferred resolution* the seventh of the dominant seventh appears in one voice, and is "transferred" to another voice within the same chord. The third inversion of the dominant seventh chord (seventh in the bass) is relatively more dissonant than are the other positions. Therefore, the seventh is rarely transferred from the bass voice in eighteenth century styles. The seventh in the bass usually resolves regularly.

Example 23—h

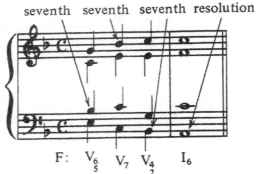

An application of the delayed and transferred resolutions is found in example 23—i.

Example 23—i

Sonata in C Major, Second Movement, K. 279   Mozart

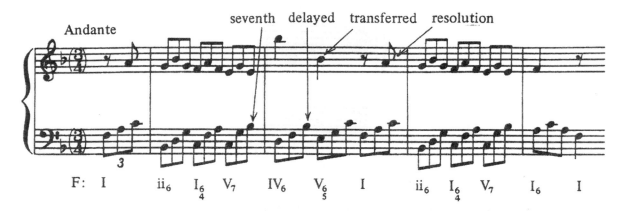

In a *bass resolution* the seventh of the dominant seventh moves up, usually scalewise, if the note of resolution appears in the bass (in any octave) in the subsequent chord.

Example 23—j

Chorale: *"Lobt Gott, ihr Christen allzugleich"*   Bach

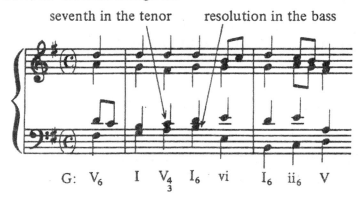

Inversions of the dominant seventh typically were written with no tone doubled and all chord members present. When chord members are omitted from seventh chords in inversion in four-part writing the result is a relatively weak vertical structure. However, seventh chords in root position may be found with the fifth omitted.

Example 23—k

First inversion with fifth omitted; not in the style.

Root position with fifth omitted; in the style.

When the complete dominant seventh is used in root position with the leading tone in the soprano, and is followed by a root position tonic triad, the tonic is characteristically incomplete (no fifth present). This allows the leading tone to resolve up and the seventh to resolve down.

Example 23–1

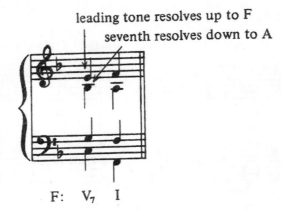

leading tone resolves up to F
seventh resolves down to A

F: V₇ I

The seventh of the V_7 typically was not doubled because of its strength as a tendency tone.

The figured bass symbols for seventh chords in various positions are shown in examples 11–b and 11–c.

Keyboard Assignment 23

a. Approach, use, and resolve (using the progression ii–V₇–I) the dominant seventh in any major or minor key of up to and including four sharps and four flats. Do not write this out, but think it out at the keyboard, employing good voice leading. The seventh chord may be in any desired position.

b. Play the following progressions in all major keys, around the circle of fifths.

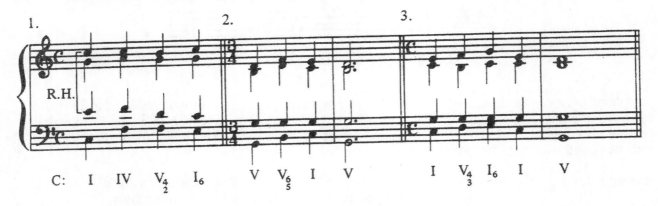

c. Play the progressions in b. above in all minor keys, around the circle of fifths.

CHAPTER 24
Motive Development, Melody, the Phrase and Period Forms

Motive Development

A motive may be defined as a small musical unit which is developed in a significant way in a musical composition. A motive may consist of an interval (two notes), or several notes, or it may be a rhythmic pattern. Example 24—a illustrates the use of a rhythmic motive which appears in several movements of a Beethoven symphony.

Example 24—a

Symphony No. 5   Beethoven

Composers use, or *develop*, motives for the purpose of achieving continuity in a musical work. They seek to achieve a balance between unity and variety through the development of motives. Developmental techniques which have evolved over several centuries include:

1. *Repetition.* This technique creates the highest degree of unity of all the developmental devices. Frequently a composer varies the repetition of a motive by the addition of notes, or by a change in rhythm, as shown in example 24—b.

Example 24—b

Sonata in B♭ Major, K. 333   Mozart

2. *Sequence.* A sequence is an immediate restatement, in the same voice, of a musical idea at a different pitch level.

Example 24–c

Phantasie, K. 475, Adagio

Mozart

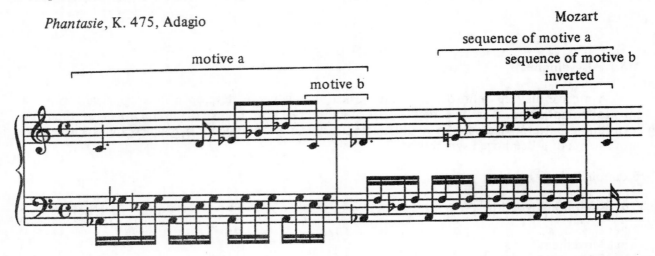

3. *Inversion.* In this technique, intervals move in the direction opposite to that occuring previously. In this type of melodic, or "mirror," inversion; intervals usually retain their general type (second, third, or fourth, etc.), but their specific type (major or minor, etc.) may vary, depending upon the harmonic progressions. Inversions may be applied to all, or to a portion of a motive, theme, or subject. For example, the sequence in example 24–c contains an inversion of the final interval, motive b. Mozart proceeds immediately to the inversion of the subject, quoted in example 24–d.

Example 24–d

Phantasie, K. 475

Mozart

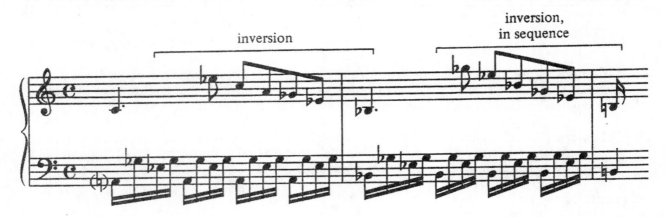

4. *Expansion or contraction of an interval.* In the sequence quoted in example 24–d, certain intervals have been expanded, and others contracted.

Example 24–e

156

5. *Diminution and augmentation.* In diminution, a musical idea is presented in smaller note values than those appearing in the original. In augmentation, a musical idea is presented in larger note values than those appearing in the original.

Example 24—f

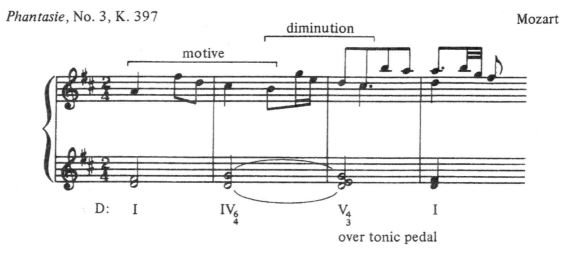

Phantasie, No. 3, K. 397   Mozart

The chorale melody in the soprano part in the cantata *"Christ lag in Todesbanden,"* example 12—c, illustrates the principle of augmentation.

6. *Rhythmic metamorphosis.* In rhythmic metamorphosis, the rhythm is altered, but the note values are not uniformly increased or decreased.

Example 24—g

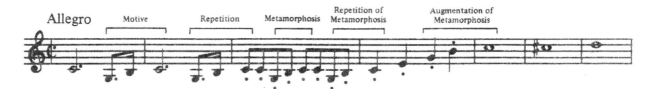

Symphony No. 1   Beethoven

7. *Imitation.* Imitation is the repetition of material in a different voice, generally at a different pitch level.

Example 24—h

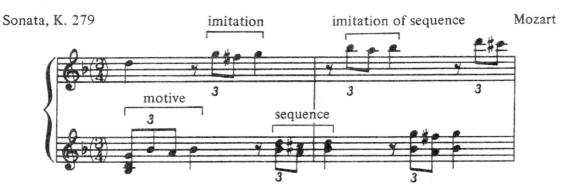

Sonata, K. 279   Mozart

Melody

Melody may be defined as a meaningful succession of tones. Although the melodic practices of the Baroque and Classic periods are extremely varied, there are certain general principles which may be observed in the work of the composers writing at that time.

In an eighteenth century musical texture, the principal melody part typically moves with a fairly well defined purpose and direction. This sense of direction is the *melodic curve*. Possible melodic curves are many and varied. Some obvious ones are:

Example 24—i

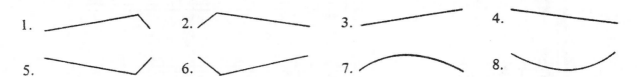

The number of measures included in each of the graphic representations in example 24—i may vary from perhaps two, to eight, or more.

Eighteenth century composers generally avoided writing melodic lines having only a few notes used repeatedly and aimlessly.

In the melodic lines of the eighteenth century, scalewise motion predominates over leaps, and small intervals occur more frequently than large intervals. When two or more leaps in the same direction occur, the notes are typically chord tones in the same harmony.

Example 24—j

Symphony No. 40, K. 550, Fourth Movement   Mozart

Leaps in one direction are frequently prepared by a scale line in the opposite direction. Likewise, leaps in one direction are often followed by a scale line in the opposite direction. Example 24—k illustrates both concepts.

Example 24—k

Sinfonia, from Cantata 156   Bach

A leap which occurs on a beat, and which has been preceded by a scale line in the same direction, is not often found in Baroque and Classic literature.

158

Example 24–l

generally outside the style

The term *homophonic*[1] denotes a musical style in which voices are treated as being of unequal melodic importance. Generally in homophonic music, a principal voice (often the upper part) is *accompanied* by other voices with less identity. The accompanimental voices are characterized by the occurence of repeated notes or arpeggiated patterns. A further characteristic of homophonic music is its organization in phrases, and in larger forms based on the phrase.

The *phrase* is a rhythmic, melodic, or harmonic structure organized so as to express a musical thought. In Classic literature, the phrase generally extends through four measures and ends with some kind of cadence.[2] The phrase is the basic structural unit in homophonic music.

The rhythmic organization of a phrase is usually one of the following types.

1. ⌢2 measures⌢ ⌢2 measures⌢

Example 24–m

Sonata in B♭ Major, K. 333, Third Movement   Mozart

B♭: I   vi   ii   V I_6 V_6 I ii_6 I_6^4 V

2. ⌢2 measures⌢ ⌢1 measure⌢ ⌢1 measure⌢   (In numbering measures, only measures having a "down-beat" are counted.)

---

[1] The other principal musical style of the Baroque and Classic periods which is in contrast to the homophonic style, is the polyphonic style, or polyphony. In polyphony, voices are generally approximately equal in melodic value. In addition, polyphonic forms, while sectional, are not characterized by period-type phrase relationships. Many eighteenth and nineteenth century compositions combine homophonic and polyphonic elements. (Polyphonic forms are beyond the scope of this text.)

[2] A rare exception is the phrase which is all one harmony (typically tonic) and; therefore, has no harmonic cadence, as in example 24–w.

Example 24–n

Minuet in G

Beethoven

G: I V_7 I

3. 1 measure 1 measure 2 measures

Example 24–o

Sonata in B♭ Major, K. 570

Mozart

Allegro

B♭:   IV I_6 V_6 I

4. 1 measure 1 measure 1 measure 1 measure

Example 24–p

Sonata in G Major, K. 283

Mozart

Allegro

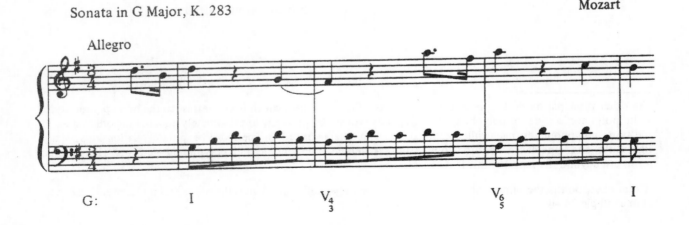

G: I V_4^3 V_5^6 I

5. 4 measures

Example 24—q

Sonata in F Major, K. 332   Mozart

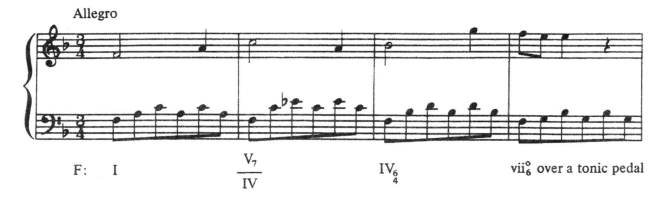

F: I $\dfrac{V_7}{IV}$ IV$_{6}^{4}$ vii$^{\circ}_{6}$ over a tonic pedal

Phrases having fewer than or more than four measures generally have a special "charm," perhaps because they are the exception to the typical practice. Phrases having more measures than four often have a sequential treatment of one or more motives, thus extending the phrase. In example 24—r, the cadence is interrupted, and two measures are repeated. *Extensions* of this type may be omitted (as a kind of structure test) with no loss to the essential musical continuity.

Example 24—r

Sonata in E♭ Major   Haydn

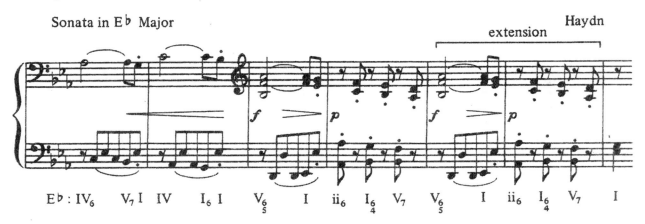

E♭: IV$_6$ V$_7$ I   IV   I$_6$ I   V$_{6}^{5}$ I   ii$_6$ I$_{6}^{4}$ V$_7$ V$_{6}^{5}$ I   ii$_6$ I$_{6}^{4}$ V$_7$ I

The *repeated phrase* is the most rudimentary of all the small "part" forms. This form is found in folk song more than in eighteenth century compositions. An example of this form is the Spanish-American folk song found in keyboard assignment 24—c.

In Classic literature, a phrase is generally followed by a second phrase which balances the first and which creates a question-answer effect between the two. This effect is enhanced by the use of a half cadence at the end of the first phrase. This small form is the *period*. The two phrases are called the *antecedent* and the *consequent*.

Example 24—s

often 4 measures	often a half cadence	often 4 measures	cadence
Antecedent Phrase		Consequent Phrase	

The thematic relationship of the two phrases may be as follows:

a. The second phrase may be essentially the same as the first, but employ a different cadence, as in example 24—t. This form is the *period with parallel phrases.*

Example 24—t

Symphony No. 9, Op. 125, Fourth Movement   Beethoven

b. The second phrase may be closely related to the first, but not so close as to be parallel construction. This form is the *period with related phrases.*

Example 24—u

Symphony No. 5   Beethoven

The second phrase may be unrelated to the first, as in example 24—v. This form is the *period with contrasting phrases.*

Example 24—v

Piano Sonata in C Minor, Op. 13, First Movement   Beethoven

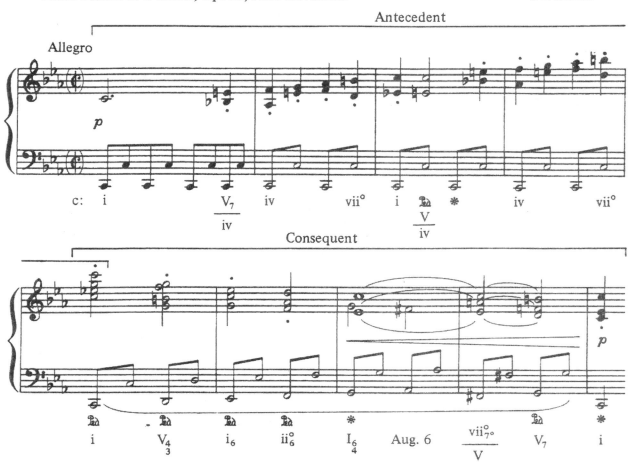

The note C in measure five is the final note of the antecedent phrase and is also the first note in the consequent phrase. The use of a note in this way produces an *elision*.

A composer may write two consequent phrases to answer the antecedent (opening) phrase. This is the *period with consequent group*.

Example 24—w

Sonata in B♭ Major, K. 570   Mozart

I V_7 I

Other Characteristics of the Classic Style

In the Classic style, *cadences*—particularly final cadences—typically involve two or three suspensions or retardations, prepared from the dominant or dominant seventh chord, sounding over the final tonic, then resolving to the tonic triad.

Example 24—x   1.   Piano Sonata, K. 279, Mozart

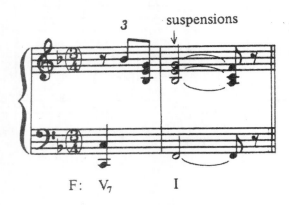

F: V_7 I

2.   Piano Sonata, K. 281, Mozart

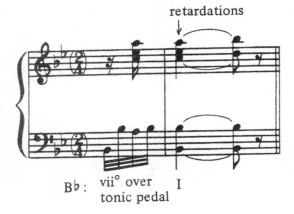

B♭:   vii° over   I
tonic pedal

A further characteristic of Classic cadences is the pattern illustrated in example 24—y. The tonic triad in second inversion resolves to a dominant seventh chord which sounds through an entire measure, and is animated by a trill on the second scale degree.

164

Example 24—y

Piano Sonata in B♭   Haydn

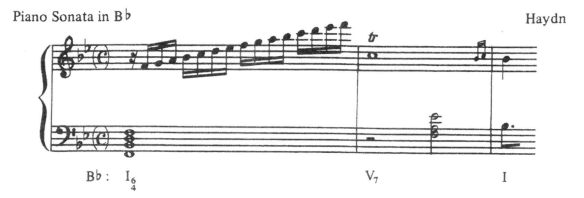

B♭:   I$_6^4$ V$_7$ I

Diminished triads are occasionally used in root position in three-voice writing. (This is also true of Baroque three-voice writing.)

Example 24—z

Piano Sonata, K. 283   Mozart

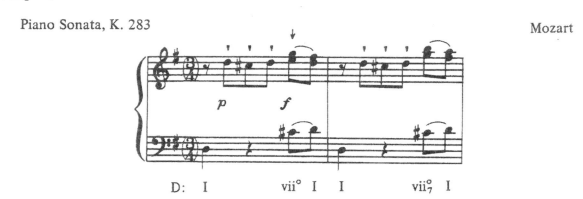

D: I   vii° I   I   vii$_7^o$ I

The melodic use of the *augmented second* interval occasionally occurs over a continuing dominant chord (V, V$_7$, vii$_6^o$, or vii$_{7\circ}^o$) in minor keys.

Example 24—aa

Piano Sonata, K. 279   Mozart

d: V$_7$ i

Example 24—bb shows some *octave* and *fifth relationships* which are not typical in Classic writing. Also shown, are some stylistically acceptable alternatives.

Example 24—bb

GENERALLY OUTSIDE THE STYLE

WITHIN THE STYLE

Keyboard Assignment 24

Harmonize the following melodies at the keyboard, with a suitable accompaniment pattern (as for group singing). A much slower harmonic rhythm should be used here than is found in four-voice chorales, so that the melodies may move forward freely. Allow for modulation. Some suggested accompaniment figures are shown. Students with limited keyboard facility should choose a pattern which will allow them to play fluently and artistically. Any portion of one of the patterns may be repeated, or omitted, as needed. Play, using the melody lines as written, without the use of any kind of chord symbols.

Suggested accompaniment patterns, illustrated in A minor.

1.

2.

3.
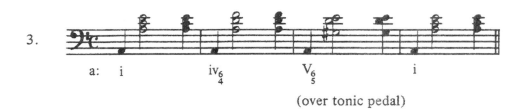

(over tonic pedal)

4.

a. German carol

b. French Folk Song

c. Spanish-American Folk Song

APPENDIX I

Music Manuscript

Note heads are not round circles. The whole-note is "shaped" from upper left to lower right.

Example I—a

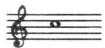

All other note heads, and sharps, flats, and naturals, are shaped from lower left to upper right.

Example I—b

The vertical lines in the sharp, flat, and natural are thin; the diagonal lines are thick.

Ledger lines are spaced the same distance apart as the lines of the staff.

Example I—c   correct   incorrect

The stem, with the note head, should extend one octave. The stem of a chord extends to the octave of the highest note if the stem is turned up, and to an octave of the lowest note if the stem is turned down. Stems may be shortened where they would otherwise merge with nearby notation or text.

Example I—d

The stem of a single note written using several leger lines reaches the middle line of the staff.

Example I—e

The stem is placed on the right side of the note head when the stem is turned up (♩), and is placed on the left side of the note head when the stem is turned down (♩). When one voice or part is written on a staff, single notes below the middle line are written with the stem up.

Example I—f

Single notes on the middle line and above are written with the stem turned down.

Example I–g

The stem should be thin.

Single eighth-notes (and sixteenth notes, etc.) are written with the flag turned in toward the note head.

Example I–h   correct   incorrect

Notes of differing values occuring on the same beat are stemmed separately.

Example I–i   correct   incorrect

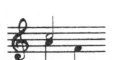 

When the interval of a second is written between two independent voices on one staff (for example, the soprano and alto parts of a chorale), the upper note is written to the left, so that the two stems are aligned vertically.

Example I–j   correct   incorrect

When the interval of a second is written on one stem, the lower note is placed to the left.

Example I–k

Chords involving whole-notes are written in this same way, as though the notes had a stem.

Example I–l

The direction of the stem for a chord is determined by the distance of the highest and lowest notes of the chord from the center staff line. If the highest note of the chord is farther from the center line than the lowest note is, the stem is turned down, and if the lowest note is farther from the center line than the highest note is, the stem is turned up.

Example I–m

The same rule is applied to determine the direction of the stems of a series of notes grouped by one or more ligatures (or beams).

Example I–n

When the highest and lowest notes of a chord are of equal distance from the center line, the stems are usually turned down.

Example I–o

Ligatures are one-half space thick. For each ligature beyond two, the stems are extended by the distance of one space.

Example I–p

Ligatures generally parallel the overall curve of the notes to which they are connected.

Example I–q

When the slant of the notes is extreme, the slant of the ligature is usually modified so that it deviates from the horizontal by only the width of one space.

Example I–r

The length of the stems is increased, not decreased, to accommodate the situation illustrated above. When the curve of the notes is ambiguous as to direction, the ligature may parallel the staff lines.

Example I–s

When accidentals precede a chord in such number that they cannot be vertically aligned, the highest accidental is placed in its normal spacing in front of the inflected note; the second highest accidental is moved to the left. Additional accidentals are moved to the left until space allows for a subsequent accidental to be vertically aligned with the highest accidental.

Example I—t

When a tie is written between single notes of one voice or part on the staff, the tie is arched opposite the stem between the note heads.

Example I—u   correct   incorrect

Ties are not placed in such a way as to come between two voices that are written on one staff.

Example I—v   correct   incorrect

Each note of a chord that is intended to be tied must be tied.

Example I—w   correct   incorrect, unless "a" and "c" are to be restruck

When an even number of notes are tied, half the notes arch over and half arch under. When an odd number of notes are tied, the natural relationship of note head to stem determines the placement of the odd numbered tie.

Example I—x

When an inflected note is tied, the accidental is not repeated unless the note tied into is the first note of a new page or score.

Example I—y   correct   incorrect

(A natural or a flat is required to avoid ambiguity.)

Accidentals should be rewritten for each octave in which the inflection is intended. The following is ambiguous, and therefore undesirable.

Example I—z

Slurs are placed opposite the stems if all the notes being slurred are stemmed the same way. If notes being slurred are not uniform in the direction of their stems, the slur is placed over the notes.

Example I—aa

A slur encompassing a tied note must include the tied note.

Example I—bb

Accents and staccato marks are placed opposite the stem unless the notes are double stemmed. Down bow and up bow markings are placed over the notes regardless of stem direction.

Example I—cc   Bowings:

In a musical score, each beat and each portion of beat is to be aligned vertically. (In order to accomplish this, it is advisable to copy the "busiest" part in each measure first.) All rests are aligned in the same manner as notes, with the exception of the whole rest. Whereas a whole *note* is aligned with the first beat of the measure, a whole *rest* is placed in the middle of the measure when it is used to indicate a whole measure of rest.

Notes are spaced approximately corresponding to their value in the score and parts.

Example I—dd   correct   incorrect

The whole rest is used to indicate a whole measure of silence in any meter, although some copyists prefer to use a breve or double whole rest in $\frac{4}{2}$ meter.

Example I—ee   or

Several measures of rest in an instrumental part are indicated as follows:

Example I—ff

Meter changes and rehearsal letters are to be *clearly* shown.

In $\frac{3}{4}$ meter, two quarter rests are used to indicate two beats of silence. The eighth rest is similarly used in $\frac{6}{8}$, $\frac{9}{8}$, and $\frac{12}{8}$.

Example I—gg

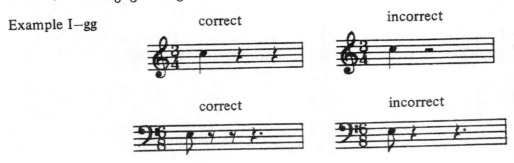

The meter signature is placed *once* at the beginning of the composition **and is** *not* **repeated at** the beginning of each new score (assuming the meter does not change). When **a meter change is** made, it *follows* the bar line.

Example I—hh

When a meter is changed at the beginning of a new score, the new meter is also placed at the end of the previous score, unenclosed by a bar line.

Example I—ii

The clef and key signature *are* written at the beginning of each score. When a key signature is changed from sharps to flats, a thin double bar is written, then the sharps are cancelled in order and the flats are written. When a key signature is changed from flats to sharps, the **double** bar is written, the flats cancelled and the sharps are written.

When a key change is to occur on a subsequent score or page, the performer is warned of the change after the light double bar and no bar line is used at the end of the staff.

Example I—jj

To change from sharps to fewer sharps or from flats to fewer flats the new signature is written (after the thin double bar) and the necessary naturals are written in order.

Example I—kk

When a clef change is made, the new clef goes *before* the bar line.

Example I—11

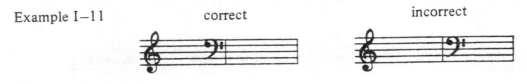

174

When a clef change is prepared at the end of a staff, the clef *is enclosed* by the final measure bar.

Example I—m

The final measure of a composition concludes with a double bar, the first bar being thin and the second thick.

Example I—nn

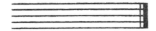

When a composer desires a section to be repeated, he encloses it with double bar-repeat signs.

Example I—oo

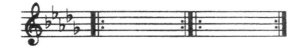

If the material to be repeated includes the first measure of the composition, the first double bar is omitted.

Allegro

Example I—pp

In instrumental music, tempo indications (allegro, a tempo, etc.) are placed at the top of the score and above the staff on individual parts. Expression marks (p, ⎯⎯⎯⎯⎯⎯ , ritard., crescendo, etc.) are placed below each part on the score affected by the change and are placed below the staff on individual parts. In choral music, all tempo and expression marks and words go above each part affected by the indication. The text of the composition is written below the staff on each part.

A musical score of two or more staves must be aligned vertically. The following example is incorrect in its placement of notes and rests in the upper two voices.

Example I—qq

The score should be aligned as follows:

Example I–rr

APPENDIX II

The Harmonic Series

The harmonic[1] series is a natural phenomenon in which the strings or columns of air in musical instruments vibrate not only as one complete whole, but also in two, three, four, or more parts. The presence or absence and relative strengths of the harmonics give each instrument its individual tone quality, or timbre (rhymes with amber). For example, the flute produces almost no overtones other than the first (the octave), and the clarinet produces the odd-numbered harmonics, etc.

The harmonic series is present in all musical tones regardless of register, but it is conveniently illustrated over a low note.

Example II—a

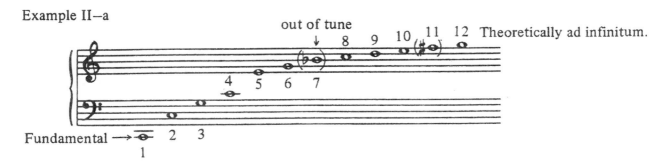

The relationship of the octave is always the ratio of 2:1, and the ratio of the perfect fifth is that of 3:2, the basis of Pythagorean tuning (sixth century B. C.). However, a series of twelve perfect fifths (to produce all the tones of the chromatic scale) tuned in this exact ratio does not return to a higher octave of the original tone, but results, instead, in a tone noticeably sharp.

There have been several systems of tuning in use at various times which attempt to compensate for this acoustical discrepancy, including:

1. Mean-tone tuning, with slightly flat fifths, perfect thirds, but unusable enharmonic equivalents.

2. Just-intonation, with perfect thirds and fifths, but having only a limited number of usable triads.

3. Equal temperament, with slightly flat fifths and sharp thirds, but with the advantage of spreading the acoustical problem evenly throughout the entire range of intervals and keys and, thus, to allow for enharmonic equivalents and for distant modulation.

Whereas none of the tones in the harmonic series over C would correspond exactly with the tuning of the tempered keyboard (except octaves of C), the seventh and eleventh harmonics are much flatter than the corresponding tempered keyboard pitches. For this reason, they are shown as special cases by being enclosed in parenthesis. The harmonic series is of immediate concern to brass players, who need an awareness of which tones in the series must be "lipped" up or down. The seventh harmonic is so flat as to be unusable on valved brass instruments and on trombone in first position.

---

[1] The chart shows the *harmonics* (also called *partials*) one through twelve, above C. The term *overtone* refers to the same series of tones, but numbered differently; the second partial (the octave) is the *first overtone*, etc.

APPENDIX III
Supplemental Rhythmic Exercises

I. Rhythmic exercises using notes larger than units, units, and divisions.

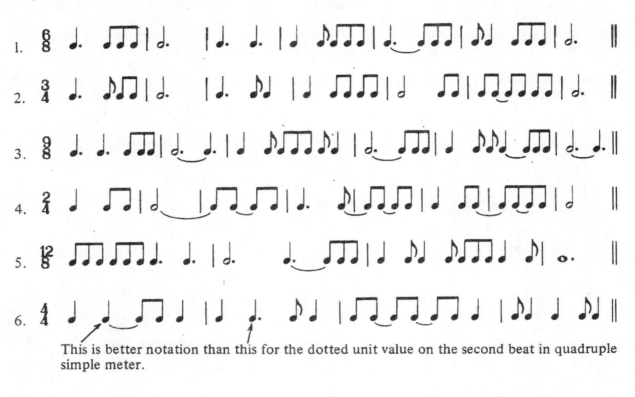

This is better notation than this for the dotted unit value on the second beat in quadruple simple meter.

13.

14.

15.

16.

17.

18.

II. Rhythmic exercises in simple and compound meter, using units, divisions and subdivisions.

1.

2.

3.

4.

5.

6.

III. Rhythmic exercises using notes larger than units; units, divisions, and sub-divisions with ties between units, and borrowed-divisions.

3. 9/8
4. 2/4
5. 12/8
6. 4/4
7. 6/16
8. 3/8
9. 9/16
10. 2/8
11. 12/16
12. 4/8
13. 6/4
14. 3/2
15. 9/4
16. 2/2

IV. Rhythmic exercises using units, divisions, sub-divisions, borrowed divisions, borrowed sub-divisions, ties, and rests.

APPENDIX IV
Atonal Ear Training Exercises

A. Major and minor seconds. Sing using letter names.

B. Seconds and thirds.

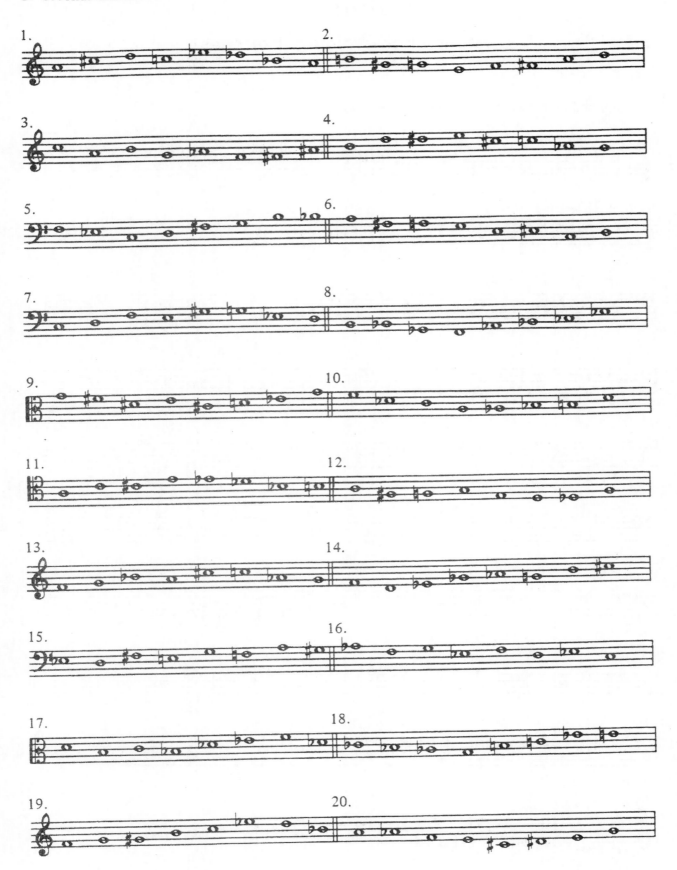

C. Seconds, thirds and the perfect fourth.

D. Seconds, thirds, perfect and augmented fourths, perfect fifths, and minor sixths.

E. All intervals within the octave.

APPENDIX V
Tonal Ear Training Exercises

These exercises are provided for student drill. Students may play these exercises for each other.

I. Ear training exercises, Chapters 1—9.

    A. Sing the following broken triad patterns with numbers. Repeat this exercise using a random selection of chord types and starting notes.

    B. Practice singing the following broken triad patterns with numbers. Repeat this exercise using a random selection of chord types and starting notes.

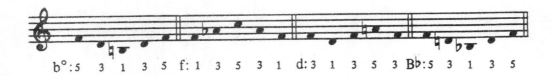

C. Position and type of isolated triads.

Determine the chord member sounding in the soprano and in the bass, by applying the correct broken triad pattern to the following triads. Solve the problem with three playings.

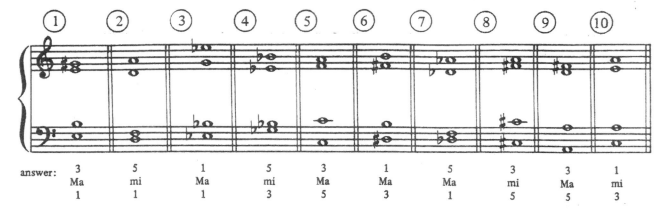

answer:
	3	5	1	5	3	1	5	3	3	1
	Ma	mi	Ma	mi	Ma	Ma	Ma	mi	Ma	mi
	1	1	1	3	5	3	1	5	5	3

D. Isolated intervals.

Each problem will be played twice melodically, and once harmonically.

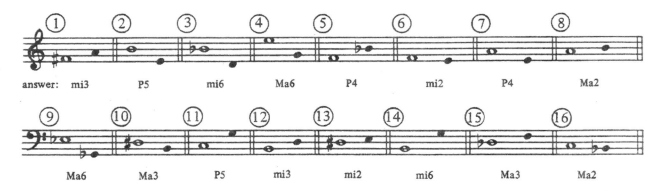

answer: mi3   P5   mi6   Ma6   P4   mi2   P4   Ma2

Ma6   Ma3   P5   mi3   mi2   mi6   Ma3   Ma2

E. Melodies without rhythm.

The following melodies will be played at a moderate tempo. The key and starting note are given to the student. Solve the problem with four playings.

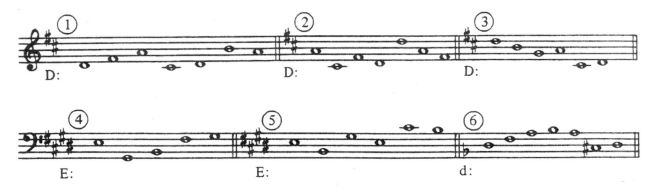

189

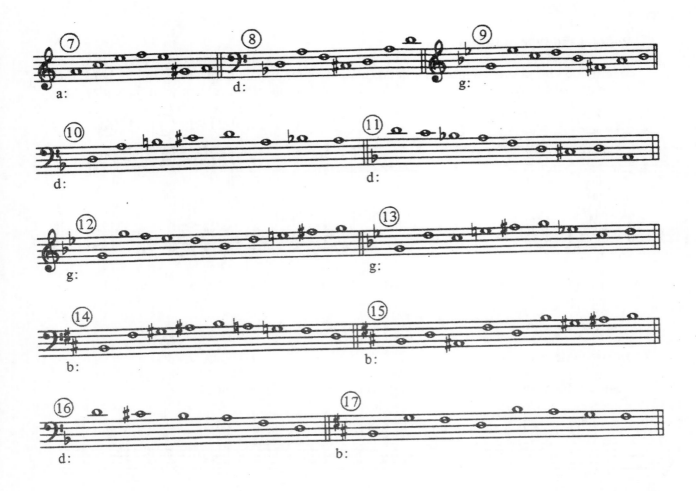

F. Eight-tone rows.

Rows from Appendix IV—A will be played. Solve the problem in three playings. Only major and minor seconds will be played. The answer is the name of each interval, not the actual notes, for example:

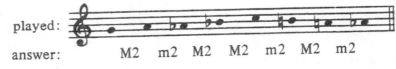

played:

answer: M2   m2   M2   M2   m2   M2   m2

ANSWERS:

1. M2 m2 M2 m2 m2 m2 M2   2. M2 m2 M2 m2 M2 M2 m2
3. M2 m2 M2 M2 m2 m2 m2   4. m2 m2 M2 m2 M2 m2 M2
5. M2 m2 M2 m2 M2 m2 M2   6. m2 M2 m2 M2 m2 m2 m2
7. M2 M2 m2 M2 m2 m2 M2   8. M2 m2 M2 m2 M2 M2 m2
9. m2 M2 m2 M2 m2 M2 M2   10. M2 m2 m2 m2 M2 m2 M2
11. M2 M2 m2 M2 M2 M2 m2   12. M2 m2 M2 m2 M2 m2 M2
13. m2 M2 m2 M2 m2 M2 M2   14. m2 M2 m2 M2 m2 M2 m2
15. M2 m2 M2 m2 M2 m2 M2   16. M2 m2 M2 m2 m2 m2 M2
17. m2 M2 M2 m2 M2 m2 M2   18. m2 m2 m2 M2 M2 m2 M2
19. M2 m2 m2 M2 m2 M2 M2   20. m2 M2 m2 m2 m2 M2 M2

G. Rhythmic Dictation. The meter signature is given and the unit is established. Solve the problem with five playings.

H. Melodic dictation. The information in the box is given to the student. Solve the problem with seven playings.

II. Ear training exercises, Chapters 10–13.

A. Isolated major, minor, and diminished triads, for position and type. Solve the problem with three playings.

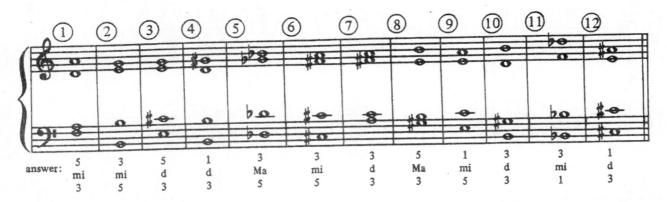

answer:
①	②	③	④	⑤	⑥	⑦	⑧	⑨	⑩	⑪	⑫
5	3	5	1	3	3	3	5	1	3	3	1
mi	mi	d	d	Ma	mi	d	Ma	mi	d	mi	d
3	5	3	3	5	5	3	3	5	3	1	3

B. Major, minor, diminished, and augmented triads, and major-minor seventh chords, for type *only*. Solve the problem with three playings.

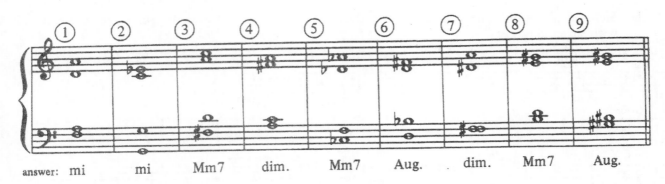

answer:
①	②	③	④	⑤	⑥	⑦	⑧	⑨
mi	mi	Mm7	dim.	Mm7	Aug.	dim.	Mm7	Aug.

C. Isolated intervals, seconds through major sevenths.

Each problem will be played twice melodically and once harmonically.

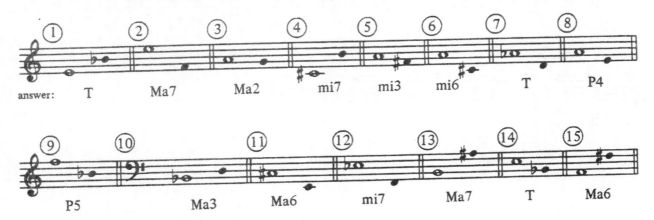

answer:
①	②	③	④	⑤	⑥	⑦	⑧
T	Ma7	Ma2	mi7	mi3	mi6	T	P4

⑨	⑩	⑪	⑫	⑬	⑭	⑮
P5	Ma3	Ma6	mi7	Ma7	T	Ma6

192

D. Eight-tone rows.

Rows from Appendix IV—B will be played. Solve the problem with three playings. Only major and minor seconds, and major and minor thirds will be played.

ANSWERS:

1. M3 m2 M2 m3 M2 m3 m2   2. m3 m2 m3 m2 m2 m3 M2
3. m3 M2 M3 m2 m3 m2 M3   4. m3 m2 m2 m3 m2 M3 m2
5. M2 m3 M2 M3 m2 M3 m2   6. m3 m2 m2 M3 m2 M3 M2
7. M2 m3 m2 M3 m2 M3 m2   8. m2 M3 m2 m3 M2 m2 M3
9. m2 m3 m2 m3 m2 m2 M3   10. M3 m2 m3 m2 M2 m2 m3
11. m3 m2 m3 m2 M2 m3 m2   12. m3 m2 M2 m3 M2 m2 M3
13. M2 m3 m2 M3 m2 M3 m2   14. m3 m2 m3 M2 m2 M3 M2
15. m2 M3 M2 m3 M2 M3 m2   16. m3 M2 M3 M2 m3 m2 m3
17. m3 m2 M2 m3 M2 M2 M3   18. m2 M2 m2 M3 m2 m3 m2
19. M2 m2 m3 m2 m3 m2 M3   20. m2 m3 m2 m3 M2 m2 m3

E. Rhythmic dictation.

Solve the problem with five playings.

193

F. Melodies without rhythm.

Solve the problem with four playings.

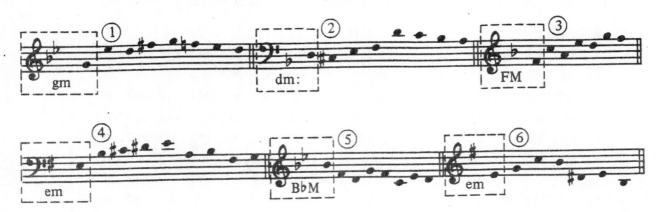

G. Melodic dictation.

Solve the problem with seven playings.

III. Ear training exercises, Chapters 14–15.

A. Isolated triads for position and type.

Repeat ear training exercise II–A, increasing the speed with which identification of triad type and position is made.

B. Isolated intervals.

Repeat ear training exercise II–C, increasing the speed with which intervals are identified.

C. Rhythmic dictation.

Solve the problem with five playings.

D. Eight-tone rows.

Rows from Appendix IV–C will be played. Solve the problem with three playings. Seconds, thirds, and the perfect fourth will be played.

ANSWERS:

1.	M2	P4	m2	P4	P4	m2	M3	2.	m3	m2	P4	m2	M2	m3	m2
3.	P4	P4	m2	m3	m2	m3	m2	4.	m2	M2	P4	P4	m2	m3	m2
5.	m3	m3	m2	M3	m2	P4	m2	6.	m2	M3	M2	m2	M2	P4	P4
7.	m2	P4	m2	P4	M2	P4	m2	8.	M2	M2	m2	P4	m2	P4	m2
9.	P4	M2	m2	m3	M2	P4	m2	10.	m2	m2	P4	M2	M3	m2	M3
11.	P4	m2	P4	m2	m3	M2	m3	12.	P4	M2	m2	M3	m2	M2	P4
13.	m3	m2	M2	P4	M2	P4	m2	14.	m3	M2	m3	m2	P4	M2	m2
15.	M3	m3	P4	m2	M3	M2	P4	16.	M2	P4	m2	m2	M3	m2	M3
17.	m3	M3	m2	P4	P4	m2	m3	18.	P4	m2	P4	m2	m3	m2	m3
19.	M3	m2	M2	M2	m2	P4	P4	20.	M3	m2	M2	P4	P4	m2	P4

195

E. Harmonic Dictation, major and minor triads in root position in major and minor keys.

Each exercise will be played slowly seven times, with emphasis on the outer voices. Steps toward solving the problems are:

1. First playing. Write the soprano line. At the same time, apply the isolated triad patterns to each successive soprano tone, determining the chord type and soprano member. For example:

2. Second playing. Write the bass line, and the bass chord member. Difficult leaps in the bass can be deduced from the isolated chord factors.

3. The inner voices can be filled in by following the principles of partwriting. Alto and tenor lines are difficult to hear when played on the piano, especially when non-harmonic tones are not present.

4. Third and fourth playing. Concentrate on the function of the chords, i.e., the tonic, dominant, and dominant triads should be recognized as such and labled with Roman numerals.

5. Final playings. Confirm your conclusions.

6. Alternative exercise: Identify only the Roman numeral analysis, in three playings.

F. Melodic dictation

Solve the problem with seven playings.

IV. Ear training exercises, Chapters 16—19.

    A. Isolated triads, for position and type.
       Repeat ear training exercise II—A, increasing in speed.

    B. Isolated intervals.
       Repeat ear training exercise II—C, increasing the speed.

    C. Rhythmic dictation.
       Solve the problem with five playings.

D. Eight-tone rows.

Rows from Appendix IV–D will be played. Solve the problem with three playings. Seconds, thirds, perfect and augmented fourths, perfect fifths and minor sixths will be played. "T" (tri-tone) indicates A4 or d5.

ANSWERS:

1. A4 P4 m2 m6 T   P5 M2   2. m3 M2 m6 P4 M2 T   M2
3. m6 m2 m3 m2 P4 m3 m2   4. m3 M2 T   T   m2 M2 P4
5. M3 M2 m6 m2 m6 P4 P4   6. P4 m2 m6 P4 P4 M2 m6
7. T   M2 P5 M2 m2 T   M2   8. M2 m2 M2 T   M2 m6 P4
9. m6 m2 M3 M2 T   M2 m6   10. m2 m3 T   P5 M2 M2 T
11. M2 m2 M3 T   M3 T   m6   12. m6 m2 T   M2 M3 P4 P4
13. M3 m2 m6 m2 m3 m2 T   14. m6 M2 P5 M2 m3 M2 M3
15. m6 M2 m2 m6 M3 m2 T   16. P4 m6 M2 M2 P5 M2 T
17. M2 T   P4 m2 T   P4 M3   18. T   M2 P5 m6 M3 M2 T
19. m3 m2 M2 T   m3 m2 P4   20. m6 P4 m2 m3 T   P4 T

E. Harmonic Dictation, major and minor keys, all triads, root position and inversion.

Solve the problem with seven playings. (Alternate exercise: Identify only the Roman numeral analysis in three playings.)

A: I vii°₆ I₆ I ii vii°₆ I   f: i III iv V VI ii°₆ V

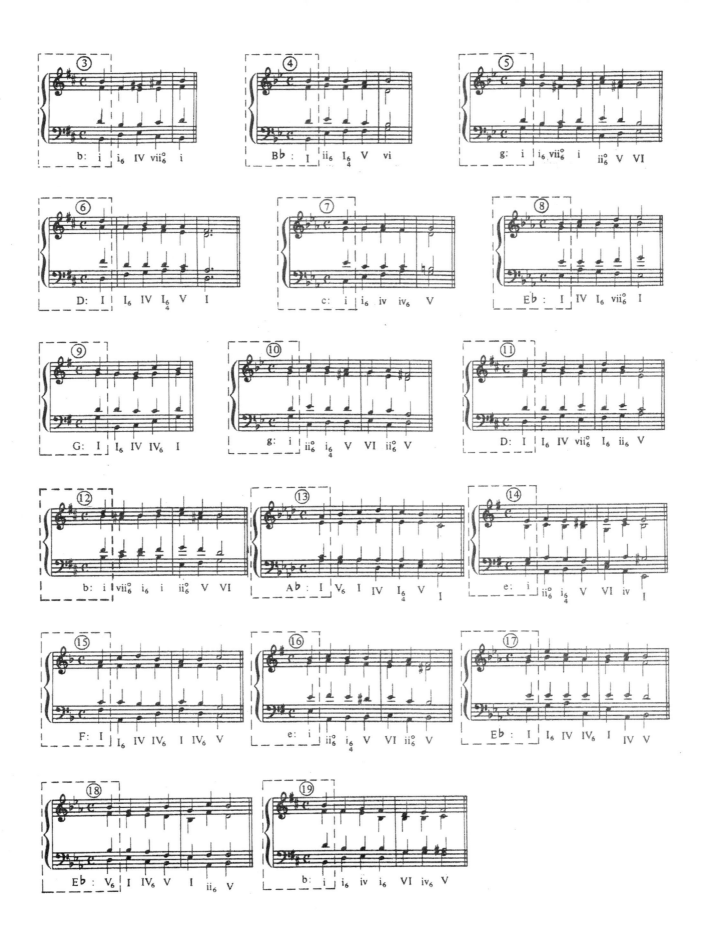

F. Melodic Dictation.

Solve the problem with seven playings.

V. Ear training exercise, Chapters 20–22.

A. Isolated triads.
Repeat ear training exercise IV–A as needed.

B. Eight-tone rows.
Repeat ear training exercise IV–D (taken from Appendix IV–D).

C. Harmonic dictation, diatonic common chord modulation.
Solve the problem with seven playings.

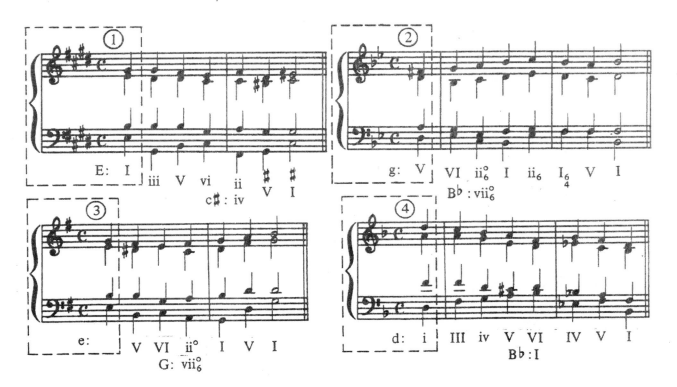

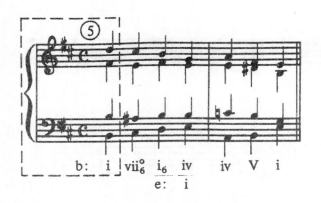

b: i | vii°₆ i₆ iv | iv V i
                    e: i

g: i | i₆ iv ii°₆ | I₆ V I
         B♭: vii°₆

D. Harmonic dictation, non-harmonic tones.

Solve the problem with seven playings.

① A.P.T. sus. sus.
E: I | V₆ I | I₆ V | I V

② sus. P.T. N.T. N.T.
g: i | V | VI ii°₆ i | V

③ E.T. sus. sus. E.T. ant.
G: I | V | vi IV | I₆ V | I

④ orn. sus. sus. ant. sus. orn.
g: i | vii°₆ | i₆ i V | i

⑤ sus. sus. sus.
F: I | V₆ | I V | vi IV | I

⑥ sus. P.T. sus. sus.
E♭: V | IV₆ V₆ I | V₆ | I V I

E. Harmonic dictation, non-harmonic tones and modulation.

Solve the problem with seven playings.

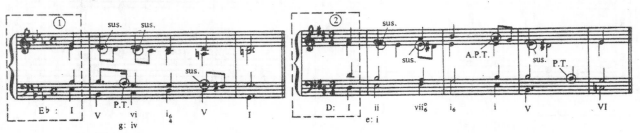

① sus. sus. sus. P.T.
E♭: I | V vi i₆₄ | V | I
         g: iv

② sus. sus. A.P.T. sus. P.T.
D: I | ii vii°₆ i₆ | i V | VI
   e: i

202

F. Melodic Dictation, modulation.

Solve the problem with seven playings.

VI. Ear training exercises, Chapters 23—24.

A. Eight-tone rows.

Rows from Appendix IV—E will be played. Solve the problem with seven playings. All intervals within the octave.

ANSWERS:

1.	M7	P4	m3	m2	m7	T	T	2.	m2	M2	M3	m6	m7	M6	M2
3.	M7	M6	m3	m2	m7	T	M3	4.	M6	m3	m2	M3	P5	M7	m3
5.	m3	m2	M2	m7	M2	m3	M6	6.	m3	m7	m2	m7	T	M6	M3
7.	m2	M7	m3	m2	M3	M2	T	8.	M2	P4	T	m7	m3	M2	m6
9.	M7	m7	m3	T	m7	T	M2	10.	T	M7	m3	T	P4	M7	m7
11.	T	M2	T	M7	T	M6	m3	12.	M2	T	m7	P4	P4	M2	P4
13.	m3	P4	T	M7	T	M2	T	14.	m2	M2	M3	M6	M2	m6	m2
15.	M3	M7	P4	M3	m3	M7	m7	16.	M7	m2	m3	M2	M7	T	M2
17.	M3	m2	M3	m2	M2	m2	M2	18.	m6	M7	M2	m3	M2	P5	M7
19.	M2	M3	m2	P5	M6	M2	m2	20.	m3	m2	m7	T	m2	T	M2

B.

Sing the following broken chord patterns for the major-minor seventh chord with numbers. Repeat this exercise using a random selection of starting notes and positions.

1 3 5 7 5 3 1 3 1 3 5 7 5 3 1 5 3 1 3 5 7 7 5 3 1

C. Position of major-minor seventh chords.

Determine the soprano and bass positions of these major-minor seventh chords by applying the appropriate broken chord pattern.

Solve the problem with three playings.

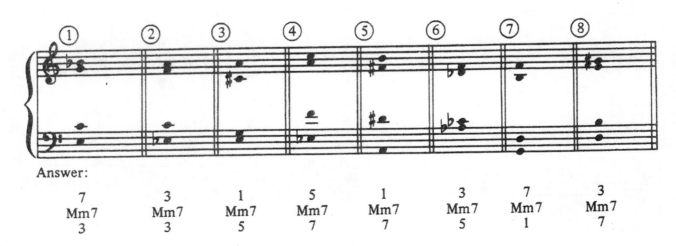

Answer:

7	3	1	5	1	3	7	3
Mm7	Mm7	Mm7	Mm7	Mm7	Mm7	Mm7	Mm7
3	3	5	7	7	5	1	7

D. Harmonic dictation, major-minor seventh chords.

Solve the problem after seven playings.

E. Melodic Dictation, phrase and period forms from Baroque and Classic literature.

Solve the problem after seven playings.

Sonata in B Minor, Scarlatti

① b:

Sonata in E Major, Scarlatti

② E:

Presto
③ D:
Brandenberg Concerto No. 4, Bach

Molto Vivace
④ e:
Sonata in E Minor, Haydn

(modulates to G)

Allegro Con Brio
⑤ C:
Symphony No. 1, Beethoven

Allegro Assai   Flute Sonata in C Minor, Telemann 
⑥ c:

Vivace   Flute Sonata in F Major, Telemann
⑦ F:

Chaconne from Partita in D Minor
for Solo Violin, Bach

Piano Sonata, Op. 10, No. 3,
Beethoven

Piano Sonata, K. 333, Mozart

Piano Sonata in E♭, Haydn

Passacaglia in C Minor, Bach

Concerto for Horn, K. 417, Mozart